# Present and Future of Artificial Intelligence
## My Approaches, Perspectives and Visions...

Md. Sadique Shaikh

**ELIVA PRESS**

ELIVA PRESS

**Md. Sadique Shaikh**

This book not only a scholarly monograph but a quick journey to future with Artificial Intelligence with my modeling, vision, forecasting, perspectives and modern approaches. All the concepts, contents and models as book write-up I wrote in very easy language to understand by one and all levels of reader's which left you speechless after reading this book. I tried my best to create full-fledged Ethiopia of Artificial Intelligence with all its positive, negative and controllable impacts lucidly. Hence the book not only for AI engineers, practitioners, researchers and designers but also for all general readers who are interested in Present and Future of Artificial Intelligence.

Published: Eliva Press SRL

Address: MD-2060, bd.Cuza-Voda, 1/4, of. 21 Chişinău, Republica Moldova

Email: info@elivapress.com

Website: www.elivapress.com

ISBN: 978-1-63648-035-0

# Present and Future of Artificial Intelligence

## My Approaches, Perspectives and Visions…

## Prof. (Dr.) Md. Sadique Shaikh

B.Sc. (ES), M.Sc. (ES), M.Tech. (IT),

D.B.M, P.G.D.M. (EM), M.B.A. (HRM),

M.B.A. (Marketing), M.Phil (Management), DMS (IMM), Ph.D. (Mgmt.)

### AIMSR

Jalgaon, M.S, India

**Dedicated to……..**

My Mother **"Shahenaaz Parvin"**

My Wife **"Safeena Sadique Shaikh"**

My loving Son **"Md. Nameer Shaikh"**

My loving Son **"Md. Shadaan Shaikh"**

Dedicated to my Close Friends

**"Tanveer Sayyed"**

# "Jyoti Firke"

# "Ritashri Chaudhari"

# Content

# About Author:

**Prof. (Dr.) Md. Sadique Shaikh**

B.Sc. (ES), M.S. (ES), M.Tech. (IT & AI),

D.B.M, P.G.D.M. (EM), M.B.A. (HRM),

M.B.A. (Marketing), M.Phil. (Management), DMS (IBM)

**AIMSR**

Jalgaon, M.S, India

Prof. Md. Sadique Shaikh presently designated as Professor and Director in Technology and Management at KYDSC Trust's Institute of Management & Sciences (IMS), Bhusawal, M.S, India. He is working for M.Tech and M.B.A courses for various subjects but few sound research domains are Robotics Vision, Machine Learning, Image Processing, Humanoid Intelligence, Bionics, Mobots, Advanced AI, International Business, Data Analytics, Bigdata Management, IoT, VO, MIS, HRIS Digital & Optical Electronics, Nanotechnology & Quantum Computing, Spintronics etc. He is qualified in M.S (ES), M.Tech (IT), M.B.A (HRM), M.B.A (MM), PGDM followed by M.Phil. Doctorate in Management Studies DMS (International Business), D.B.M and Pursuing Ph.D. He has delivered Invited Talk, Short Communication, Keynote Speeches and presented research work in several reputed places like IITs, IIMs, BARC, NMU, PU, MU, NU are few of them. He has 15 years of experience in industries and Academics presented work more than 123 conferences/symposiums and authored 61 international books and more than 124 research papers, short communication, opinions and research reports worldwide some of them Germany, U.K, U.S.A, India, Malaysia, Mauritius, Hong Kong, Singapore, U.A.E, Italy, France, Japan, China, Romania, Spain and Australia in the fields of Robotics, Bionic Brain, AAI, UAI, Quantum

Computing, Information Technology, Medical & Surgical Robotics, Space Science, Management, Cosmology & Space Science and Electronics Sciences. **His 09 books republished in Italian, Spanish, Portuguese, Polish, Swedish, Dutch, German, French, Russian and English 09 different international languages worldwide by Omniscriptum Berlin, Germany and others Publishing houses worldwide and the book "Next Level Vision in Artificial Intelligence" and "Business of Different Thinking" most popular in them.** He is guiding to many students for advanced research project in Technology and Management. He is editorial board member in several esteemed International journals of U.K, U.S.A, Japan, and India. Worked in several International Conferences/Symposiums as OCM & Advisory Committee Member of U.S.A, U.K, Australia, Japan, Spain, India and Turkey. Organized several National/International conferences/symposiums, summit, MDPs, LDPs and FDPs and several big events. He is reviewer of several reputed international journals (REAJ) Robotics & Automation Engineering Journal is one of them. **Became Chief Guest Editor of special volume of journal "Medical Robotics and Surgery".** Reviewer and Member in Journal of medical and pharmacy. Editor in Invasive Surgical Research Journal and expert in Advanced Medical Robotics. He has written several invited short communication/Interviews and editorial for world reputed journals. He is International Educator, Author and Invited Speaker. He is OCM of Bio-Core, Dubai, U.A.E. He is Editor of OMICS Online London, SciPG, U.S.A and Research-Route Journal, India, JARAP-India and likewise several. He is reviewer of Kosmospublishers, USA. He is invited speaker in ICEAAE-2019 (Frankfurt, Germany) 2nd Edition of Aerospace and Aeronautical Engineering. Editorial Board Member of Journal of Robotics & Automation" and "Journal of Mechanical Handling and Automation" of JournalPub, Noida, India. Editorial Board Member of Journal of Applied Sciences, Redelve LLC Pub., USA. Became Editorial Board Member in International Journal of Robotics and Automation, International Journal of Mechanical Handling and Automation JournalspPub, India, Became EDM in "Asian Journal of Social Science Management & Economics" India. He is OCM of INTERNATIONAL CONFERENCE ON PHARMACOLOGY AND PHARMA NETWORK, 26-28 September 2019, Hilton Garden Inn Houston Westbelt Houston, USA. He is OCM in International Conference on Artificial Intelligence & Machine Learning, Osaka, Japan. Became Editorial Board member in "Asian Journal of Social Science Management & Economics" India, International Multilingual Journal of Science and Technology (IMJST), Berlin, Germany. Speaker and OCM in International Conference on Artificial Intelligence & Machine Learning ,OSAKA, JAPAN, "International Conference on Mechanical & Aerospace Engineering" Tokyo, Japan and " World Physics Congress" Dubai, U.A.E. OCM in International Scientific Summit in Artificial Intelligence and Robotics, Valencia, Spain, OCM in International Conference on Robotics and Automation Engineering, Roma, Italy. Reviewer in Journal of Multidisciplinary Engineering Science Studies (JMESS), Berlin, Germany. Chief Editor International Journals of research Publications (IJR Publications). Chief Editor of MAA International Journal of Research in Computer Applications and Technology, Indore, India. Work in advanced A.I selected at Paris, USA, Japan, Spain, Hong Kong, London, Brazil, Indonesia, Germany, UAE, and so on. Became OCM in International Conference on Physics and Network Malaysia 2019, Kuala Lumpur,

Malaysia. Became OCM in 3$^{rd}$ International Conference & Expo on Aerospace and Unmanned Arial Systems: Taking the Sky Streets Aviation-The Next Level, Philadelphia, U.S.A. He is Leading Committee Member in World Congress on Automobile, Mechanical and Industrial Engineering (WCAMIE-2019), Berlin, Germany. **Designated as Lead Guest Editor of SciencePG USA for American Journal of Management Science and Engineering and designed special issue "Artificial Intelligence for Future Business".** He received "Best Leadership Award" from Today- Research & Ratings. **He received IOSRD Best Researcher Award 2018 at Panduchary and VDGOOD Outstanding Scientist Award 2019 at Bangalore, India**. He has finished two self-help books entitled "What I am is Thinking" and "Saturations" contracted to publish with Penguin Publication, New Delhi. He is Associative Editor of GPH-Journal of Business Management, Haryana, India. He is EBM in International Journal of Current Science and Multidisciplinary Research, India. (Management and Economics Section), India. He is EBM of International Journal of Advancements in Technology, LongDom Publishing, Belgium. He is OCM in AMME-2020 Summit at Dubai. Reviewer of Oriental Journal of Computer Science and Technology (OJCST), India. Active member of VDGood Scientific Association. Won **RULA Awards** organizes by World Research Congress for **International Research Award in AI,** Trichy, T.N, and India. Won **"Distinguished Scientist Award"** from VDGood Association in Chennai, India. Became OCM and Speaker in GAVIN "2nd International Conference on Advanced Artificial Intelligence & Robotics" 28-29 July 2020 at Berlin, Germany. Became OCM and Speaker in Artificial Intelligence, Machine Learning and Data Science, 01-02 December 2020, Bucharest, Romania as well as . Became OCM and Speaker in Robotics and Computer Science World Forum" to be held in Lisbon, Portugal from November 09-10, 2020. OCM and Invited Speaker of 4th World Conference on Robotics and Artificial Intelligence, December 17-18, 2020 | Istanbul, Turkey. He is OCM and webinar speaker with talk "AI and Singularity" at 2nd International Robotics and Automation Engineering Conference August 3-4, 2020 - Paris, France. Received (International Society for Scientific Network) **ISSN International Award** in ISSN Scientific & Research Awards 2020 as **"Innovative Researcher in Technology and Management"** at Madurai, India. Received **RULA International Research Ratana Award** from World Research Council (WRC) and Research Under Literal Access (RULA) as **"Innovative Scientist in Artificial Intelligence"** of the year 2020. Became Advisory Board Member of ACTA Scientific Computer Sciences Journal. He is Technical Program Committee Member of WiCOM 2020, Xi'an, China. He is OCM in Emerging Trends in Robotics and Recent Advancements in A.I at Saint Petersburg, Russia held on June 24-26 2021. Delivered Invited talk on AI and Singualarity near and post impact of COVID on Global Business & Economy likewise subjects. He is invited speaker in 3rd World Conference on Robotics and Artificial Intelligence, June 24-26, 2021, Saint Petersburg, Russia. He has reviewed more than 135 research papers for verious reputed National and international journals world wide. He is program committee member in 8th international conference on computational science and engineering (CSE-2020), 12-13 December at Dubai, UAE. He is OCM and speaker in **3rd World Conference On Robotics And Artificial Intelligence June 24-26, 2021 | Saint Petersburg, Russia. He Editorial Board Member of**

Journal of Automobiles and Automobiles Technology, France. He has recently honored with "Man of Excellence Award" in Indian Achievers Award from Indian Achievers Forum (IAF) and Ministry of Education and Information Technology, Govt. of India. He is received "Most Ambitious Researcher of The Year 2020 Award" from under Golden Research Prize from ISSN Award 2020.

**Also Visit:**

**Amazon author page:** https://www.amazon.com/Dr.-Mohd-Sadique-Shaikh-Anwar/e/B07ZRCMQMT

**Institute page:** www.imssakegaon.org/ProfSadiqueShaikh.htm

**LinkedIn page:** https://www.linkedin.com/in/dr-sadique-shaikh-29784186

This page left intentionally blank in memory of my

Late Mother "Shahenaaz Parveen"

And

My friend Late "Naziya Khan"

# Episode One: Defining Virtual Humanoid Robotics with Modeling

I have no doubt to state Virtual Humanoid Robots (VHRs) are the ultimate level of Artificial Intelligence which change the scenario of world and human technologies, it would be applicable in all domains of technology with common factor Ultra Artificial Intelligence (UAI) with disappear and appear ability by any means which boost to our civilization from Type-0 to type-1 civilization at least and would be first step to compete with Aliens technology, if exist (hypothesis only). I would like to define term Virtual Humanoid Robotics (VHR) as **"it's Humanoid Robotics with UAI and has ability to transform from Physical to Virtual by any Internal (Humanoid Self-Control) or External (Human-Control) mode activation mechanism"**. VHR is future technology which will use energy from Sun (or Space), Internet of Things (IoT) with RFID USN, Bigdata and Self-learning and healing mechanism. Now I would like to generate future utopia front of your eyes with initial modeling to coined term VHR in this short communication.

**Keywords:** Humanoid Robotics, Bionic Brain, UAI, Virtual Humanoid Robotics, Robotics Teleportation.

**Modeling to VHR:**

### 1) VHR-Basic Engineering Model:

I depicted in my first model "VHR-Basic Engineering" that there we need to extent our fundamental engineering aspect of Humanoid to Virtual Humanoid robotics domain. Hence model divided into two broad chambers as Humanoid Chamber and to give virtual ability Virtualization chamber. As we can analyze from model for successful humanoid building we need advanced Humanoid robotics hardware's which link to Bionic Brain as similar to human brain mimic in the form of UAI which further cascade to Advanced Humanoid Operating System and Communication Interfaces. After successful engineering of first segment successful physical humanoid can build but to next level i.e. to convert physical humanoid into virtual and back from virtual to physical we doesn't need to modify hardware but to strongly need to give extension to existed. Hence

Virtualization chamber exhibits this regard in model. The virtualization chamber has two functional blocks to engineer Advanced Physical to Virtual Mode transfer Units and Light/Projection/Optical/Teleport interfaces Engineering.

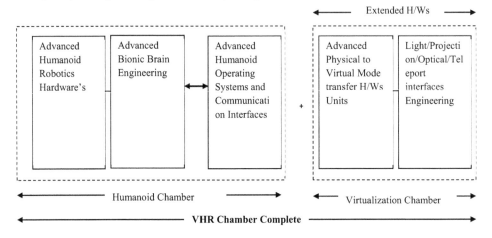

**Source:** Prof. Md. Sadique Shaikh

### 2) Physical-to-Virtual Modes Switch Model:

My second purposed model "Physical-to-Virtual Mode Switch" model one of the essential VHR engineering models, in another word can say expansion and detail discussion on Virtualization Chamber second part of my first model. Its lucid and clear representation of concept in model diagram I considered three different possible modes viz. M1, M2 and M3 which may be increase in future with technological advancement and new methods of virtualization. The mode M1 has highest priority to implement VHR where Humanoid hardware itself has ability to appear and disappear itself with self-control (Internal Control) which is only hypothesis right now. The second mode M2 has possible and second priority Teleportation and lot research going on this Mode M2 by several premium university and institutions scholars. The last mode M3 is easiest one but not satisfactory where virtualization engineer using virtual and augmented reality.

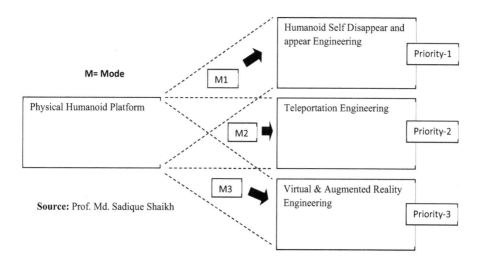

**M= Mode**

Physical Humanoid Platform

Source: Prof. Md. Sadique Shaikh

M1 → Humanoid Self Disappear and appear Engineering — Priority-1

M2 → Teleportation Engineering — Priority-2

M3 → Virtual & Augmented Reality Engineering — Priority-3

## Conclusion:

I have discussed two models and with the help of them try to learn one of the promising and world change future technology "Virtual Humanoid Robotics" where Humanoid not only seems to be like human in near future but also will have ability to Avatar itself. This would be very helpful to send humanoid virtually in deep-space, on stars and planets to understand universe closely with teleportation or internal humanoid mechanism. VHR also ultimate level of AI hence might be shift mankind race on planet earth from Type-0 civilization to Type-1 civilization as shown in sci-fi movies.

## Acknowledgement

I would like to credit this work to my loving wife Safeena Khan, my angels Md. Nameer Shaikh, Md. Shadaan Shaikh and my close friend Tanveer Sayyed.

# References

1) Md. Sadique Shaikh, " Analysis and modeling of Strong A.I to engineer BIONIC brain for humanoid robotics application" in American Journal of Embedded System and Applications, Published by Science Publishing Group, October 2013, vol.1, No.2, doi:10.11648/ajesa.20130102.11, New York, America (U.S.A)(paper available at URL:www.sciencepublishinggroup.com/j/ajesa )

2) Md. Sadique Shaikh, "Ultra Artificial Intelligence (UAI): Redefing AI fir New Research Dimension" in Advanced Robotics & Automation (ARA), OMICS International, London, April 2017, Pgs.1-3, ISSN No: 2168-9695, Vol. 6, Issue. 2, DOI: 10.4172/2168-9695.100063. (Paper available online at URL: www.omicsonline.com

3) Md. Sadique Shaikh, "Fundamental Engineering for Brain-Computer Interfacing (BCI): Initiative for Neuron-Command Operating Devices" in Computational Biology and Bioinformatics (CBB), SciencePG, U.S.A, November 2017, Pgs. 50-56, Vol. 5, No. 4, DOI: 10.11648/j.cbb.201770504.12, (Paper available online at URL: www.sciencepublishinggroup.com/j/cbb )

4) Md. Sadique Shaikh, Defining ultra artificial intelligence (UAI) implementation using bionic (biological-like-electronics) brain engineering insight. *MOJ App Bio Biomech.* 2018;2(2):127–128. DOI: 10.15406/mojabb.2018.02.00054

5) Md Sadique Shaikh. Insight Artificial to Cyborg Intelligence Modeling. Arch Ind Engg: 1(1): 1- 5.

6) "Artificial Intelligence Engineering for Cyborg Technology Implementation" in Robotics & Automation Engineering Journal , Robot Autom Eng J. 2018; 3(1): 555604, U.S.A (Paper available at https://juniperpublishers.com/)

3. Md. Sadique Shaikh, "Ultra Artificial Intelligence (UAI): Redefing AI fir New Research Dimension" in Advanced Robotics & Automation (ARA), OMICS International, London, April 2017, Pgs.1-3, ISSN No: 2168-9695, Vol. 6, Issue. 2, DOI: 10.4172/2168-9695.100063. (Paper available online at URL: www.omicsonline.com

4. Md. Sadique Shaikh, "Fundamental Engineering for Brain-Computer Interfacing (BCI): Initiative for Neuron-Command Operating Devices" in Computational Biology and Bioinformatics (CBB), SciencePG, U.S.A, November 2017, Pgs. 50-56, Vol. 5, No. 4, DOI: 10.11648/j.cbb.201770504.12, (Paper available online at URL: www.sciencepublishinggroup/j/cbb )

5. Md. Sadique Shaikh, Defining ultra artificial intelligence (UAI) implementation using bionic (biological-like-electronics) brain engineering insight. *MOJ App Bio Biomech.* 2018;2(2):127–128. DOI: 10.15406/mojabb.2018.02.00054

# Episode Four: Insight Artificial to Cyborg Intelligence Modeling

**Abstract:** today Artificial Intelligence play vital role to everyday changing and made easy to human life advance automation, but more than of it is Cyborg Intelligence where instead of machine mankind themselves can able to make extreme powerful with implementing and interfacing artificial/Bionic parts with their biological organs and those work together. Hence I have shown in my short communication how one can move for Cyborg Intelligence from artificial intelligence and what are the commons and what are the different to set engineering skills in it.

**Keywords:** Artificial Intelligence, Humanoid, Bionic, Cyborg, Cyborg Intelligence.

## 1. Introduction:

As humans live longer there is a growing need for availability of organs for transplant however shortage in donations necessitates the development of artificial alternatives with AI often called "Bionic". Advances in medicine have led to the availability of artificial blood, replacement joints, heart valves, and heart-lung machines that are common implanted using AI for Bionic organs. One of the primary and utilitarian goals of artificial intelligence research is to develop machines with human-like intelligence. Great progress has been made since the start of AI as a field of study. One dominating research paradigm in AI has been based on the assumption that various aspects of human intelligence can be described and understood well enough to the extent that it can be simulated by computer programs through smart representational frameworks and generic reasoning mechanisms. Now a day's fusion take place Biological beings and computer systems share some common physical foundations. Communication in both biological nervous systems and computer systems, for example, depends on electrical signals. Yet, the gap between these two classes of vastly different systems is obvious and bridge with "Cyborg Intelligence".

Since researchers and practitioners confused between Bionic/AI and Cyborg, let me clear in last attempt to it. As I discussed already Bionic is biological functions, methods, systems and procedures mimic electronically with neuron interfacing but Cyborg is another possibility in Medical Robotics domains. Cyborg "Cybernetic organism" is a being with both organic and Biomechatronic body parts using which human can increase their power in all means and branch of study is "Cyborgology".

## 2. Modeling:

### 2.1. Engineering Shift Model:

This is my first interesting model named "Engineering Shift Model" and with help of this model I would like to discuss how Cyborg Intelligence (C.I) engineering issues are different as compare to Artificial Intelligence (AI). In this model I exhibit two geometries as rectangle having the four engineering corners A1, A2, A3 and A4 representing to AI engineering and Diamond inside the rectangle having four quadrants B1, B2, B3 and B4 representing to CI engineering. This model not only display issues but how engineering requirements with mapping change from AI to CI with arrow lines A1-to-B1, A2-to-B2, A3-to-B3 and A4-to-B4 equivalently. At A1 study of neuroscience require to mimic AI electronically but at B1 along with neuroscience complete human biology and anatomy need to study for proper Cyborg Intelligence development and implementation. At B2 engineering is need to design interfaces to established electronic to electronic communication but at B2 paradigm shift and need to design interfaces to establish electronic to biological and vise versa communication between biological organs and electronics parts with exchange ions- electrons. At A3 control processing engineering need to design to control overall AI electronically, but at B3 situation is different need to carry Control & Processing Engineering for NI controlled AI. Happen is like this just because of Master-Salve relation of engineering at A4 changed at B4. At A4 in AI itself Master intelligence buy at B4 Artificial Intelligence cascade with Natural Intelligence (Biological Brain) hence NI become Master intelligence and AI become slave intelligence in engineering issues of Cyborg technology implementation.

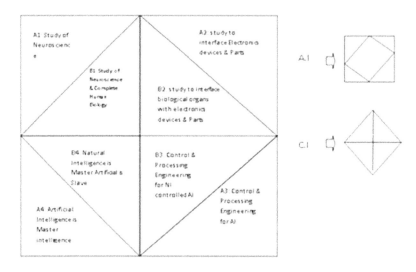

Source: Prof. Md. Sadique Shaikh

**Figure 1: Engineering Shift Model**

## 2.2. Parallel Engineering Model:

This is my second model labeled as "Parallel Engineering Model" when fusion of AI and CI engineering take place. As display in model two parallel tracks with four tiers Upside for AI engineering with L1, L2, L3 and L4 where as at downside for CI engineering with L1', L2', L3' and L4' respectively. At L1 image processing engineering considered and slightly change in case of CI at L1' as image processing and biologically synching engineering need. At L2 Natural Language Processing analysis, design and development are the issues which are extended as NLP with Artificial Language Processing (ALP) must need because not only human to computer but computer to human machine code must be encode and decode by biological brain. At L3 engineering essential is electronic interface design and simultaneously at L3' Biological-Electronics interfaces design for ions-electrons command and signaling for communication. At

essential module and Hardware essential module with further segmentation into three parts of each. Both the modules and their sub-modules have further lots of depth for DeepMind engineering. Here I am not showing technical aspects in detail but would like to show direction of engineering with DLEM.

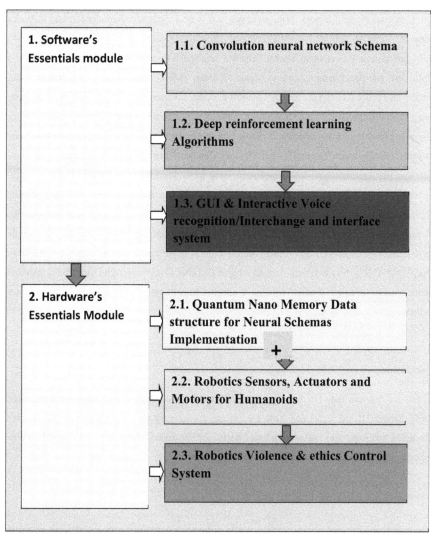

It clearly display in above model both modules need to engineer individually but must be full interactive and suitable to each other to show human-like or more then of Human-like intelligence with proper Avatar and appearance. Software essential module has three important engineering domains are Convolution neural network Schema, Deep reinforcement learning Algorithms , GUI & Interactive Voice recognition/Interchange and interface system and Hardware essential module has Quantum Nano Memory Data structure for Neural Schemas Implementation, Robotics Sensors, Actuators and Motors for Humanoids, Robotics Violence & ethics Control System. In Software module Convolution Neural Schemas must need to engineer those has capability and ability of self-programming and learning, at Deep enforcement learning algorithms super intelligence procedure and process design to fit in neural schemas for self learning system whereas using Human-Like GUI, Voice recognition, interaction and interchange voice command and voice response possible to/from DeepMind robots. The Second important modeling need is Hardware essential module where Quantum Nano Memory Data structure  design and fabricated for Neural Schemas Implementation with ultra high processing speed this is we can say DeepMind and Neural Schemas in it make it alive with super or ultra AI can say Bionic Brain. The next phase engineering is precision sensors, actuators and motors engineering for human like movements and appearance in humanoid. The last engineering phase is most important aspect as I mentioned Google developed AI-God and Church which volatile natural beliefs of human and one day might be DeepMind AI like this made their own AI religion and ethics which would be harmful for mankind hence need to precise Robotics Violence & ethics Control System to save human from robotics violence.

### Conclusion

In above communication I had discussed about DeepMind, its concepts with current examples and using Model DLEM explained how DeepMind engineering possible to carried out. I have discussed two important engineering aspects with further expansion as well also focused on how robotics violence and ethics control system is important.

## Acknowledgement

I would like to credit this work to my loving wife Safeena Khan, my angel Md. Nameer Shaikh and my close friend Tanveer Sayyed as well as our Director Dr.B.N.Gupta.

## References

1) Md. Sadique Shaikh, " Analysis and modeling of Strong A.I to engineer BIONIC brain for humanoid robotics application" in American Journal of Embedded System and Applications, Published by Science Publishing Group, October 2013, vol.1, No.2, doi:10.11648/ajesa.20130102.11, New York, America (U.S.A)(paper available at URL:www.sciencepublishinggroup.com/j/ajesa )

2) Md. Sadique Shaikh, "Ultra Artificial Intelligence (UAI): Redefing AI fir New Research Dimension" in Advanced Robotics & Automation (ARA), OMICS International, London, April 2017, Pgs.1-3, ISSN No: 2168-9695, Vol. 6, Issue. 2, DOI: 10.4172/2168-9695.100063. (Paper available online at URL: www.omicsonline.com

3) Md. Sadique Shaikh, "Fundamental Engineering for Brain-Computer Interfacing (BCI): Initiative for Neuron-Command Operating Devices" in Computational Biology and Bioinformatics (CBB), SciencePG, U.S.A, November 2017, Pgs. 50-56, Vol. 5, No. 4, DOI: 10.11648/j.cbb.201770504.12, (Paper available online at URL: www.sciencepublishinggroup/j/cbb )

4) Md. Sadique Shaikh, Defining ultra artificial intelligence (UAI) implementation using bionic (biological-like-electronics) brain engineering insight. *MOJ App Bio Biomech.* 2018;2(2):127–128. DOI: 10.15406/mojabb.2018.02.00054

5) Md Sadique Shaikh. Insight Artificial to Cyborg Intelligence Modeling. Arch Ind Engg: 1(1): 1- 5.

6) "Artificial Intelligence Engineering for Cyborg Technology Implementation" in Robotics & Automation Engineering Journal , Robot AutomEng J. 2018; 3(1): 555604, U.S.A (Paper available at https://juniperpublishers.com/)

7) "Engineering Insight for Humanoid Robotics Emotions and Violence with Reference to "System Error 1378" in Robot Autom Eng J 3(2): RAEJ.MS.ID.5555610 (2018), USA

8) "Defining Cyborg Intelligence for Medical andSuper-Human Domains" in Trends in Technical & Scientific Research, Volume 2 Issue 3 - July 2018, Trends Tech Sci Res. 2018; 2(3): 555588. Pgs. 001-002 (Available on https://juniperpublishers.com/)

9) "Ultra artificial intelligence (UAI) engineering for robotics violence control, detect and corrective measures" in International Robotics & Automation Journal, Int Rob Auto J. 2018; 4(4):242–243, DOI: 10.15406/iratj.2018.04.00129, (Available at http://medcraveonline.com)

# Episode Six: Ultra Artificial Intelligence (UAI) Engineering for Robotics Violence Control, Detect and Corrective Measures in Humanoid

**Introduction:**

What kinds of social relationships can people have with computers are there activities that computers can engage in that actively draw people into relationships with them. What are the potential benefits to the people who participate in these human-computer relationships? To address these questions researchers introduces a theory of Relational Agents, which are computational artifacts designed to build and maintain long-term, social-emotional relationships with their users. These can be purely software humanoid animated agents--as developed in this work but they can also be non-humanoid or embodied in various physical forms, from robots, to pets, to jewelry, clothing, hand-held's, and other interactive devices. Central to the notion of relationship is that it is a persistent construct, spanning multiple interactions; thus, Relational Agents are explicitly designed to remember past history and manage future expectations in their interactions with users. Finally, relationships are fundamentally social and emotional, and detailed knowledge of human social psychology with a particular emphasis on the role of affect--must be incorporated into these agents if they are to effectively leverage the mechanisms of human social cognition in order to build relationships in the most natural manner possible. People build relationships primarily through the use of language, and primarily within the context of face-to-face conversation. Embodied Conversational Agents--anthropomorphic computer characters that emulate the experience of face-to-face conversation--thus provide the substrate for this work, and so the relational activities provided by the theory will primarily be specific types of verbal and nonverbal conversational behaviors used by people to negotiate and maintain relationships. This article is also intend if level of Artificial Intelligence reach over Natural Intelligence (Human Intelligence), what would be happen, if System Error 1378 (AI malfunction error) occur one day .i.e. robotic violence due to human like emotion in Robots/Humanoid.

**Keywords:** Humanoid, Robotics Emotions, Robotics Violence, System Error 1378

**Modeling:**

I am showing here how we can engineer Humanoid in future to save it from violence with present example "System Error 1378" but which only good to understand the concepts lot of errors possibilities and malfunctions possible when Humanoid become most advanced Robot with self-learning and programming. Presently I am working on initial stage to avoid and troubleshoot robotics violence in humanoid with Counseling and shielding program unit but possibilities many more what I mentioned these are few. We need to implement precise monitoring system which default and forever active component with Humanoid execution for all tasks to trace system error 1378 and detect and informed if occur as shown in model. If system error 1378 occurred for robotics violence or war what defense engineering possible I have exhibits with four "Alternate" engineering as Alt-1, Alt-2, Alt-3 and Alt-4. These alternate engineering aspects become more to most complicated and challenging as moving from Alt-1 to Alt-4 as well as must need to engineer when robotic violence in Humanoid become more to most worst and out of control to handle and tackle properly. At Alt-1 we can design software modules to control Robotic Violence with "Counseling and Shielding" program, where as in Alt-2 as I display we need to designed Subroutines which scan system error 1378 and deactivate/disable module/part in humanoid which malfunctioning and caused to Robotic violence in Alt-3. When situation is most danger and out of control than must have to make provision in Humanoid engineering with Alt-4 "self-destruction" program but this is not cost effective and losses in terms of million dollars.

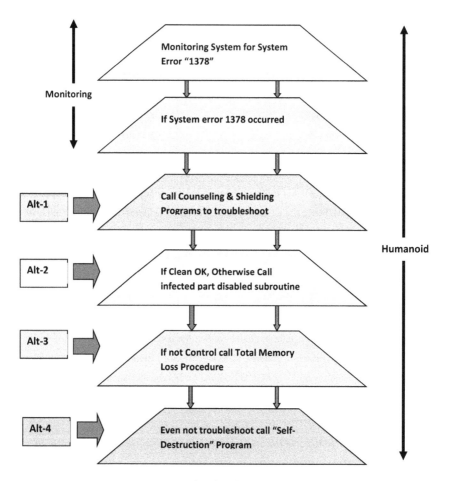

Source: Prof. Md. Sadique Shaikh

**Conclusion:**

When Artificial Intelligence become extreme advanced and over human Natural Intelligence that day seems to be dooms like days for human race even you can competently take example of Google has made Artificial Robot God and Church which against of human ethics as in subject of debate on several international news channels and you search the on internet also. Hence to protect human race from humanoid robots is one of the most important engineering issue how we can control robots and robots shouldn't have to control us and protect planet earth from robotics violence as I discussed with my modeling. Someone might be raised quotation as why I mentioned only the solution "Self-Destruction" is the provision to control robotic violence at saturation level, because if we used erase neural schema still basic booting identity module we need to initialize humanoid again because its AI, hence chance to self-recall like rebirth where as auto-system shutdown means device in sleeping mode when its turn on again it has same initialization in ANN Schemas with violence.

**Acknowledgment:**

I really thankful to my wife Safeena Shaikh for her moral support my son Md. Nameer Shaikh for his love which keeps me fresh with new ideas and my close friend Tanvir Sayyed for her positive support with me and my motivator Dr. B.N.Gupta for his constant support.

**References:**

1. NSF/EC Understanding on Co-operation in Information Technologies - Strategic Research Workshops IST-1999-12077

2. Md. Sadique Shaikh, " Analysis and modeling of Strong A.I to engineer BIONIC brain for humanoid robotics application" in American Journal of Embedded System and Applications, Published by Science Publishing Group, October 2013, vol.1, No.2,

doi:10.11648/ajesa.20130102.11, New York, America (U.S.A)(paper available at URL:www.sciencepublishinggroup.com/j/ajesa )

3. Md. Sadique Shaikh, "Ultra Artificial Intelligence (UAI): Redefing AI fir New Research Dimension" in Advanced Robotics & Automation (ARA), OMICS International, London, April 2017, Pgs.1-3, ISSN No: 2168-9695, Vol. 6, Issue. 2, DOI: 10.4172/2168-9695.100063. (Paper available online at URL: www.omicsonline.com

4. Md. Sadique Shaikh, "Fundamental Engineering for Brain-Computer Interfacing (BCI): Initiative for Neuron-Command Operating Devices" in Computational Biology and Bioinformatics (CBB), SciencePG, U.S.A, November 2017, Pgs. 50-56, Vol. 5, No. 4, DOI: 10.11648/j.cbb.201770504.12, (Paper available online at URL: www.sciencepublishinggroup/j/cbb )

5. Md. Sadique Shaikh, Defining ultra artificial intelligence (UAI) implementation using bionic (biological-like-electronics) brain engineering insight. *MOJ App Bio Biomech.* 2018;2(2):127–128. DOI: 10.15406/mojabb.2018.02.00054

6. Md Sadique Shaikh. Insight Artificial to Cyborg Intelligence Modeling. Arch Ind Engg: 1(1): 1- 5.

# Episode Seven: Artificial Intelligence Engineering for Cyborg Technology Implementation

## 1. Introduction:

As humans live longer there is a growing need for availability of organs for transplant however shortage in donations necessitates the development of artificial alternatives with AI often called "Bionic". Advances in medicine have led to the availability of artificial blood, replacement joints, heart valves, and heart-lung machines that are common implanted using AI for Bionic organs. One of the primary and utilitarian goals of artificial intelligence research is to develop machines with human-like intelligence. Great progress has been made since the start of AI as a field of study. One dominating research paradigm in AI has been based on the assumption that various aspects of human intelligence can be described and understood well enough to the extent that it can be simulated by computer programs through smart representational frameworks and generic reasoning mechanisms. Now a day's fusion take place Biological beings and computer systems share some common physical foundations. Communication in both biological nervous systems and computer systems, for example, depends on electrical signals. Yet, the gap between these two classes of vastly different systems is obvious and bridge with "Cyborg Intelligence".

Since researchers and practitioners confused between Bionic/AI and Cyborg, let me clear in last attempt to it. As I discussed already Bionic is biological functions, methods, systems and procedures mimic electronically with neuron interfacing but Cyborg is another possibility in Medical Robotics domains. Cyborg "**Cybernetic organism**" is a being with both organic and Biomechatronic body parts using which human can increase their power in all means and branch of study is "Cyborgology".

## 2. Modeling:

### 2.1. Cyborg Analysis Design (CAD) model:

This is first model and with the help of this display I want to clarify the fundamental analysis and designing issues for Cyborg engineering. This model based on four tiers 1 to 4 with further split each stage Analysis domain and Design domain. At first stage detail studies need to carry of Neuroscience theory to analyzed Cyborg with intention what you want to engineer and in design

domain design Cyborg interfaces accordingly. At the stage two researchers have to study very first human biology and anatomy and functions of biological organs to interface and synch with Cybermatic parts and at design domain devices engineer and fabricated accordingly. At stage three studies of bio-membranes, tissues, cells and anatomy have to make to design "Brain Computer Interfaces (BCI)" with ions-electrons commands and signals exchange to establish communication between biological and electronic system. In last stage bio-potential and how to interface ions with electronic devices need to carry to engineer "Neuron Command Operating Devices (NCOD)" /Cybermatic devices.

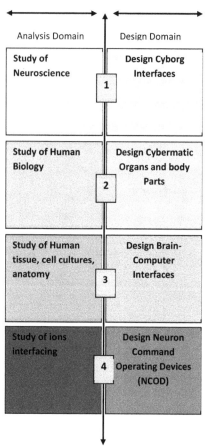

**Source: Prof. Md. Sadique Shaikh**

## 2.2. Cyborg Interface Support Model:

In continuation of first model this is second exhibit "Cyborg Interface and Support" engineering model to implement Cyborg Intelligence. It is based on four criterions with further division into two domains.

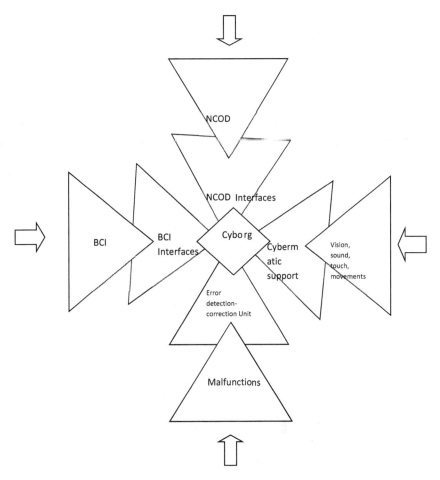

**Source: Prof. Md. Sadique Shaikh**

Instead of sequential it is random model but covered four most important designing issues to implement Cyborg Intelligence (CI). We need to design strong Brain Computer Interface with depth BCI engineering and how to synch biological system with electronic system in short precise system engineering need. Another aspect is How to design Neuron Command Operating Devices (NCOD) and how to interface NCOD with biological system. Next important thing is how to analyze and design Vision, Sound, touch and Movements with NCOD for Cybermatic support engineering. The last important engineering issue which we can not neglect, since Cybermatic devices 24 hours functional with human body lot of chances of malfunction due to continuous processing hence "Error detection and correction" engineering is important for continuous accurate error free working.

**Conclusion:**

With the help of this short communication I tried to understand what engineering parameters and steps are important and where have to change from routine AI engineering for Cyborg technology implementation with discussing two models Cyborg Analysis Designing model and Cyborg Interfaces Support model lucidly.

**Acknowledgment:**

I really thankful to my wife Safeena Shaikh for her moral support my son Md. Nameer Shaikh for his love which keeps me fresh with new ideas and my close friend Tanvir Sayyed for her positive support with me and my motivator Dr. B.N.Gupta for his constant support.

**References:**

1. NSF/EC Understanding on Co-operation in Information Technologies - Strategic Research Workshops IST-1999-12077

2. Md. Sadique Shaikh, " Analysis and modeling of Strong A.I to engineer BIONIC brain for humanoid robotics application" in American Journal of Embedded System and Applications, Published by Science Publishing Group, October 2013, vol.1, No.2, doi:10.11648/ajesa.20130102.11, New York, America (U.S.A)(paper available at URL:www.sciencepublishinggroup.com/j/ajesa )

3. Md. Sadique Shaikh, "Ultra Artificial Intelligence (UAI): Redefing AI fir New Research Dimension" in Advanced Robotics & Automation (ARA), OMICS International, London, April 2017, Pgs.1-3, ISSN No: 2168-9695, Vol. 6, Issue. 2, DOI: 10.4172/2168-9695.100063. (Paper available online at URL: www.omicsonline.com

4. Md. Sadique Shaikh, "Fundamental Engineering for Brain-Computer Interfacing (BCI): Initiative for Neuron-Command Operating Devices" in Computational Biology and Bioinformatics (CBB), SciencePG, U.S.A, November 2017, Pgs. 50-56, Vol. 5, No. 4, DOI: 10.11648/j.cbb.201770504.12, (Paper available online at URL: www.sciencepublishinggroup/j/cbb )

5. Md. Sadique Shaikh, Defining ultra artificial intelligence (UAI) implementation using bionic (biological-like-electronics) brain engineering insight. *MOJ App Bio Biomech.* 2018;2(2):127–128. DOI: 10.15406/mojabb.2018.02.00054

# Episode Eight: Modeling of Bionic Brain for Humanoid Robotics

## Abstract

Bionic Brain Engineering using Ultra artificial Intelligence (UAI) like Natural Intelligence (NI) for Humanoid became one of the biggest research areas in the field of AI and Robotics. Hence for human-like intelligence human brain mimic electronically strongly required called "Bionic" Biological like Electronic Brain with mapping and engineering exactly Natural Intelligence NI (God made) into Artificial Intelligence AI (Man made). In this direction I have developed and discussed two models "Bionic Diamond" and "Bionic Brain Engineering Model" in this article.

**Keywords:** Bionic Brain, UAI, AI, NI, Bionic Diamond, Bionic Brain engineering Model

## 1. Bionic:

*BIONICS* is a common term for bio-inspired information technology, typically including three types of systems, namely:

• bio-morphic (eg neuromorphic) and bio-inspired electronic/optical devices,
• autonomous artificial sensor-processor-activator prostheses and various devices built into the human body, and
• living-artificial interactive symbioses, e.g. brain-controlled devices or robots.

In spite of some restrictive use of the term 'bionics' in popular culture, as well as the unfulfilled promises in the fields of neural networks, artificial intelligence, soft computing and other 'oversold' areas, it was agreed that the name *bionics* as defined above is the right one for the emergent technology also described as bio-inspired information technology (some people are suggesting *info-bionics*). There are numerous programs at several funding agencies which are supporting parts of this field under various other names [1, 5].

## 2. Bionic Brain:

Bionic Brain stand for " Biological-like-Electronic" Brain with Mimic Natural Intelligence, Artificially on Silicon Chip which gives similar functioning to Humanoid (Human like Robots) like Biological Brain of human being (Refer my complete paper mentioned in reference no.2 for depth).

## 3. Modeling:

### 3.1. Bionic Diamond:

This is my first purposed model using which I want to understand to young researchers what are very important at fundamental level engineering in Bionic Brain for Humanoid as shown in Bionic Diamond. It is based on four essential parameters are Image & perception processing engineering to engineer human like sensation using artificial cognition. The second is Natural language Processing (NLP) as similar like human being with proper interpretation and lexical. Another two important aspects are self-learning and development engineering with short/long term memory management units.

Figure 1: Bionic Diamond

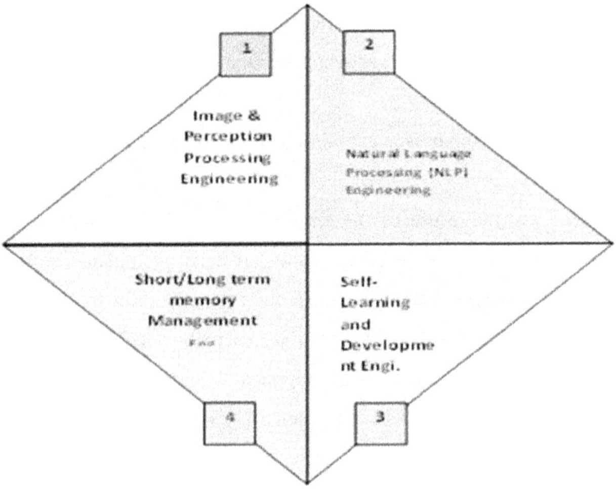

Source: Prof. Md. Sadique Shaikh

### 3.2. Bionic Brain Engineering Model:

In above exhibit I display four important domains Sensations, Processing, decision, retrieve and references and actuation for Bionic Brain Modeling with classified each into two sub criteria's. The first designing issue is sensation split as Cognition and sensors & transducers engineering for biological/environmental inputs with precise calibrations. Processing is further segmented to carry engineering on two factors intelligence and UAI-CPUs array which the main brain of overall humanoid. At third level Decision, recall, retrieve and references engineering required with Long/Short term memory management and at forth for responsiveness and human-like action from humanoid genuine engineering need   at actuation with two domains Actuators and motors engineering and behaviour & Movement engineering.

Figure 2: Bionic Brain Engineering Model

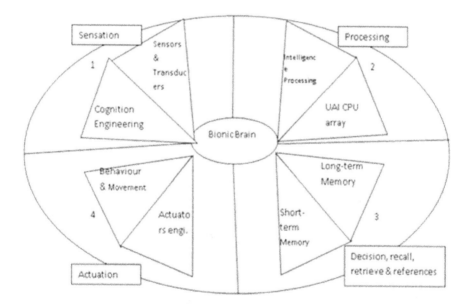

Source: Prof. Md. Sadique Shaikh

## 4. Conclusion:

In present paper I discussed very lucidly how we can analyzed and engineer Bionic Brain using UAI like NI with help of Bionic Diamond and Bionic Brain Engineering Model. This piece of research would be very useful who want to start research in the direction of Bionic Brain, Humanoid and Ultra Artificial Intelligence (UAI).

## Acknowledgment:

I really thankful to my wife Safeena Shaikh for her moral support my son Md. Nameer Shaikh for his love which keeps me fresh with new ideas and my close friend Tanvir Sayyed for her positive support with me and my motivator Dr. B.N.Gupta for his constant support.

## References:

6.  NSF/EC Understanding on Co-operation in Information Technologies - Strategic Research Workshops IST-1999-12077

7.  Md. Sadique Shaikh, " Analysis and modeling of Strong A.I to engineer BIONIC brain for humanoid robotics application" in American Journal of Embedded System and Applications, Published by Science Publishing Group, October 2013, vol.1, No.2, doi:10.11648/ajesa.20130102.11, New York, America (U.S.A)(paper available at URL:www.sciencepublishinggroup.com/j/ajesa )

8.  Md. Sadique Shaikh, "Ultra Artificial Intelligence (UAI): Redefining AI fir New Research Dimension" in Advanced Robotics & Automation (ARA), OMICS International, London, April 2017, Pgs.1-3, ISSN No: 2168-9695, Vol. 6, Issue. 2, DOI: 10.4172/2168-9695.100063. (Paper available online at URL: www.omicsonline.com

9.  Md. Sadique Shaikh, "Fundamental Engineering for Brain-Computer Interfacing (BCI): Initiative for Neuron-Command Operating Devices" in Computational Biology and Bioinformatics (CBB), SciencePG, U.S.A, November 2017, Pgs. 50-56, Vol. 5, No. 4,

DOI: 10.11648/j.cbb.201770504.12, (Paper available online at URL: www.sciencepublishinggroup/j/cbb )

10. Md. Sadique Shaikh, Defining ultra artificial intelligence (UAI) implementation using bionic (biological-like-electronics) brain engineering insight. *MOJ App Bio Biomech.* 2018;2(2):127–128. DOI: 10.15406/mojabb.2018.02.00054

11. Md Sadique Shaikh. Insight Artificial to Cyborg Intelligence Modeling. Arch Ind Engg: 1(1): 1- 5.

# Episode Nine: Defining Ultra Artificial Intelligence (UAI) Implementation Using Bionic (Biological-Like-Electronics) Brain Engineering Insight

## 1. Bionic:

*BIONICS* is a common term for bio-inspired information technology, typically including three types of systems, namely:

• bio-morphic (eg neuromorphic) and bio-inspired electronic/optical devices,
• autonomous artificial sensor-processor-activator prostheses and various devices built into the human body, and
• living-artificial interactive symbioses, e.g. brain-controlled devices or robots.

In spite of some restrictive use of the term 'bionics' in popular culture, as well as the unfulfilled promises in the fields of neural networks, artificial intelligence, soft computing and other 'oversold' areas, it was agreed that the name *bionics* as defined above is the right one for the emergent technology also described as bio-inspired information technology (some people are suggesting *info-bionics*). There are numerous programs at several funding agencies which are supporting parts of this field under various other names [1].

## 2. Bionic Brain:

Bionic Brain stand for " Biological-like-Electronic" Brain with Mimic Natural Intelligence, Artificially on Silicon Chip which gives similar functioning to Humanoid (Human like Robots) like Biological Brain of human being (Refer my complete paper mentioned in reference no.2 for depth).

Scientists are beginning to look much more closely at the mechanisms of the brain and the way it learns, evolves and develops intelligence from a sense of being conscious (Aleksander, 2002). For example, AI software designers are beginning to team up with cognitive psychologists and use cognitive science concepts. Another example centers upon the work of the 'connectionists' who draw attention to computer architecture , arguing that the arrangement of most symbolic AI programs is fundamentally incapable of exhibiting the essential characteristics of intelligence to any useful degree. As an alternative, connectionists aim to develop AI t rough artificial neural networks (ANNs). Based on the structure of the nervous system, these 'computational-cognitive models' are designed to exhibit some form of learning and 'common-sense' by drawing links between meanings (Hsiung, 2002). ANNs, then, work in a similar fashion to the brain: as information comes in, connections among processing nodes are either strengthened (if the new evidence is consistent) or weakened (if the link seems false) (Khan, 2002).The emergence of ANNs reflects an underlying paradigm change within the AI research community and, as a result, such systems have undeniably received much attention of late. However, regardless of their success in creating interest, the fact remains that ANNs have not nearly been able to replace symbolic AI. As Grosz and Davis (1994) remark: *'[Symbolic AI has] produced the technology that underlies the few thousand knowledge-based expert systems used in industry today.'* A major challenge for the next decade, then, is to significantly extend this foundation to make possible new kinds of high-impact application systems. A second major challenge will be to ensure that AI continues to integrate with related areas of computing research and other fields (Doyle and Dean, 1996). For example, the kinds of developments described for nanotechnology may go some way to accelerating progress in AI, particularly through the sensor interface. For these reasons, the list of main research areas that follows should be regarded as neither exhaustive nor clear-cut. Indeed, future categorizations will again c

## 3. Modelling:

### 3.1. Bionic Brain Classified Engineering (BBCE) Model:

This is the first purposed "Bionic Brain Classified Engineering (BBCE)" model through which I would like to focus on major engineering domains of Bionic Brain. The concept exhibit in BBCE-Model with classified Bionic Brain engineering with fundamental issue that, what you want to engineer using UAI. Because it very essential need to know though you are design in domain of Bionic Brain, the point here to discuss fundamentally two kinds of Bionic Brain engineering in present research scenario possible, one is "Mimic Bionic Brain" and another is " Born-Child like Bionic Brain". The first one Bionic Brain research in progress in several countries and also in use at initial level in some places, but the second one still need to overcome with several new concepts and engineering ideas to build up domain. I coined terms Mimic Bionic Brain as here AI engineering take place to study some genius intelligence using biological Neuroscience theory and his Natural Intelligence (NI- God made) coped electronically on Chip as Artificial Intelligence (AI-Man made) where as Born-Child like Bionic Brain would be engineering to develop completely blank electronic brain, off course similar like human brain structure but its not mimic its develop itself just like new born child who scanned environment, develop perception generate meaning and memorize identified all objects with proper communications by all means. I further discussed in my first model most generic engineering skills need to develop such Born-Child like Bionic Brain with discussing hardware's and software's modules requirements as for Mimic Bionic Brain are Advanced Machine Learning System & Mimic ANN (Artificial Neural Network) Schema Engineering at Hardware side and Advanced Artificial Intelligence Programs & Logic Program modules fit to Neural Schema on Software's side. The Born-Child like Bionic Brain also need same factors but with extension as Advanced Self Machine Learning System & Blank to self develops ANN Schema Engineering at Hardware's side whereas Ultra Artificial Intelligence (UAI) programs & Logic Program modules search to fit Neural Schemas at software's side. In hardware and software sides in both Bionic Brain in all four quadrants again vast subject to engineering.

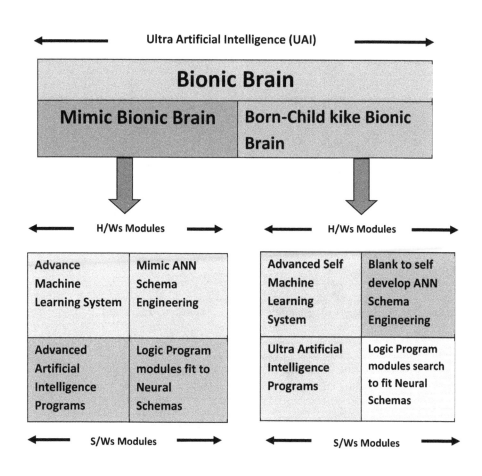

Source: Prof. Md. Sadique Shaikh

**3.2. Bionic Brain Engineering Insight (BBEI) Model:**

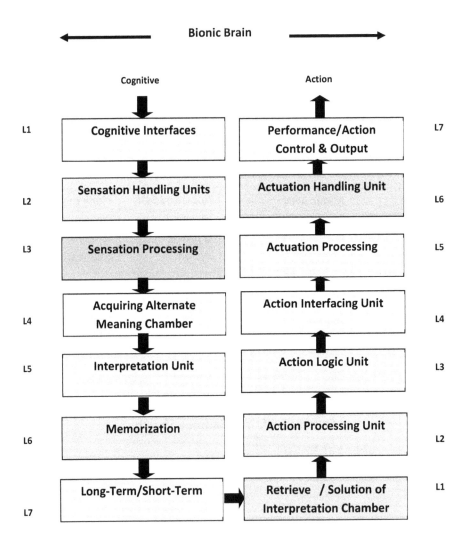

Source: Prof. Md. Sadique Shaikh

This my second designed model labeled Bionic Brain Engineering Insight (BBEI) Model which gives you rapid idea how Bionic Brain Engineer, what factors and criterions must consider while engineering and how that engineering will work in integration. This model is completely based on first one with functional engineering description in details. Hence name given Engineering Insight, here complete model split into two segments one is "Cognitive" and another is "Action" having seven layers L1 to L7 for both. In working we can assume same human brain functioning analogically to understand idea. After senses, cognition of environmental stimuli at layer L1 .i.e. Cognitive Interface in electronic volume using sensors and transducers its fed to L2 Sensation Handling Unit to filter and channelized from where pass to Sensation Processing to clarify things, elements, visuals, sounds and objects by Biological-Like-Electronic (Bionic) Brain at L3 and send to Alternate Meaning Chamber to acquire meanings at L4. From L4 its passes trough L5 Interpreter Unit to make things .i.e. information to intelligence conversion and this input to assembly Memorization often called store/restoration at L6 with attachment L7 Long-Term/Short term memories for different memorization purpose. Whole process begins from top to bottom with L1 to L7. Where as in reverse at L1 Retrieve/Solutions of Interpreter Chamber which make up and concise intelligence for action taking and output performance from Bionic Brain fed to L2 Action Processing Unit to put it in ready state from where goes Action Logic Unit layer L3 where performance strategies and scheduling of action with time control done. The assembly further input to L4 Action Interfacing Unit to prepare and ready signals for Humanoid Actuators to come in movement according to command and for this L5 & L6 Actuation Processing and Actuation Handling Unit works together from where all mechanism given to Performance/Action Control & Output at L7 to out Human-Like performance/action by Humanoid using Bionic Brain Buildup Ultra Artificial Intelligence.

**Conclusion:**

With closing this short communication I would like to conclude "Bionic Brain" is the future of Artificial Intelligence at peak level I coined term "Ultra Artificial Intelligence" here for the same. Using Bionic Brain not only possibilities for human-like/Humanoid Robots, but also Medical Robots, Space Robots for precise space research. One day Bionic Brain and Biological Brain both become tough on each other. The second challenge after this how emotion, feelings, body language, gesture, posture and expression possible to program and control using Bionic Brain in

Humanoid. At this stage there is also possibility Robotic Violence with Mankind. I have shown with help of two models how one can start journey towards it.

**References:**

1. NSF/EC Understanding on Co-operation in Information Technologies - Strategic Research Workshops IST-1999-12077

2. Md. Sadique Shaikh, " Analysis and modeling of Strong A.I to engineer BIONIC brain for humanoid robotics application" in American Journal of Embedded System and Applications, Published by Science Publishing Group, October 2013, vol.1, No.2, doi:10.11648/ajesa.20130102.11, New York, America (U.S.A)(paper available at URL:www.sciencepublishinggroup.com/j/ajesa )

# Episode Ten: Insight into Bio inspired Robotics

**Abstract**

I am trying to understand whole family of Biology and Synthetic Biology inspired robotics through this piece of communication. Broadly with assuming their sub categories in them I would like classify bio inspired robotics in to five major heads are Cyborg, Cylons, Softrobotics, Continuum-robotics, Plantoids and Nanobots. Where Softrobots and Plantoids are quite new and interesting domains of new future of AI in many forms with advanced features. This opinion gives in your notice all about them.

**Keywords:** Synthetic Biology, Cyborg, Cylons, Softrobotics, Continuum-robotics, Plantoids, Nanobots.

**Bio-Inspired Robotics Model**

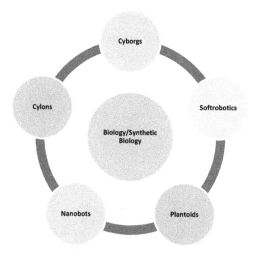

**Source:** Prof. Md. Sadique Shaikh

Biology and Synthetic Biology based Robotics segmented into five types as Cylon, Cyborg, Plantoid, Nanobot and Softrobot and all are different from each other.

**Plantoids:**

Very interesting and my concern oriented bio inspired robotics domain is Plantoid. A Plantoid is the plant equivalent of an android or humanoid with UAI can say it is a robot or synthetic organism designed to look, act and grow like a plant having advanced humanoid/Android like Artificial Intelligence. Plantoids based on key technology called "Blockchain". Plantoid is an autonomous blockchain-based life-form that is able to reproduce itself. It is a hybrid creature that lives both in the physical world mode because as a mechanical contraption made up of recycled steel and electronics and in Virtual/digital world mode because as software deployed on top of a blockchain-based network. Hence ability of Physical-Virtual-Mode switching. Plantoids would be strange and useful brach of bio inspired robotics in near future with many life-forms, intelligence forms and self reproduction forms with possible application coverage. These Blockchain based lifeforms will base on self replicating creatures.

**Softrobotics**

Soft Robotics is emerging fresh sub field in Robotics which is very useful in medical, industry, space exploration, deep sea exploration, Nano-robotics and many more likewise applications. The major benefit of Soft Robots as compare to Rigid Robots their excellent flexibility and adaptability to accomplish task. Before to move further I would like to state Soft or Continuum Robots first "Soft Robots are small, medium and big shapes various biological or non-biological body forms robots which are made up using ultra soft and flexible materials, where materials are engineered using Continuum Mechanics and Kinematics". The big difference between conventional rigid robots and soft robots, in rigid robotics intelligence engineered using AI only to control robotics body, but in soft robotics the materials using which robots has made themselves smart and has intelligence, sensations and actuations. Therefore Soft Robots can also learn from surrounding environment in self mode as well as has greater flexibility in clutching, climbing, moving, defending etc.

**Nanobots**

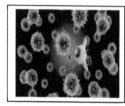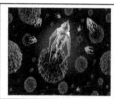

Nanbots (Nano-robots) are the robots engineered at nano sacle using Nanotechnology at atomic, cellular, molecular levels. Nanobots are also called as nanomachines, nanorobots, nanomites, nanites or nanoids etc. Research in progress about Nanobots and when got success they are would be very useful of Human body treatments, to kill bacterias, viruses, and harmful cells, like HIV, Cancer etc inside human body. These would be tiny motors and machine injected in body to kill diseases. Hence Nanobots very useful in medical field often called Nanobots as Nanomedicines. Nanobots form using Nanoparticles, quantum particles, quntum dots at $10^{-9}$ Sacle.

**Cyborgs:**

First get to know what is a Cyborg? It's an organism that has both organic ("natural" GOD made) and cybernetic ("machine" Electro-Mechanical Artificial and Man Made) parts engineered, implemented and cascaded in Human body for Biological medical assistance or to change ordinary human potentials, capacities and intelligence to super or ultra power levels. In other words, when people become Cyborg, they're part human and part machine.Cyborg is another possibility in Medical as well as super artificial power domains. Cyborg "**Cy**bernetic **org**anism" is a being with both <u>organic</u> and <u>Biomechatronic</u> body parts using which human can increase their power in all means and branch of study is "Cyborgology".

**Cylons**

Cylons are seems to be similar like Cyborg but they has big different and let me clear what they are. Cylon specially engineered for Wars and like purposes and completely made up with regular materials only human intelligence and mimic used here, whereas Cyborg engineered or implemented in human for various purposes and partly used biological or Synthetic Biological materials. This branch has less scope and attention for research due to the rapid success in Cyborgs.

**Conclusion**

Bio inspired robotics forms will change facet of world and handle routine task of mankind. These intelligence forms would be engineer and available in various sizes, forms, skills, abilities and advance features like Plantoids, Softrobots, Nanobots and Cyborgs I explained with the help of Bio Inspired Robotics Model.

**Acknowledgement**

I would like to credit this work to my loving wife Safeena Khan, my angels Md. Nameer Shaikh, Md. Shadaan Shaikh and my close friend Tanveer Sayyed.

# Episode Eleven: Communiqué on "Robotics Medical Support System (RMSS)"

## Abstract

Now days Internet of Things became very successful and peak communication network technology which can connect all possible living non-living objects, creatures and robots with each other with their unique RFID and hence my thinking started with this vision how can robotics and IoT we can merge for mankind benefits and overcome with the concept of "Robotics Medical Support System (RMSS)".

**Keywords**: IoT, IoUT, RMSS, AI, Medical Robotics

**Robotics Medical Support System (RMSS) Model**

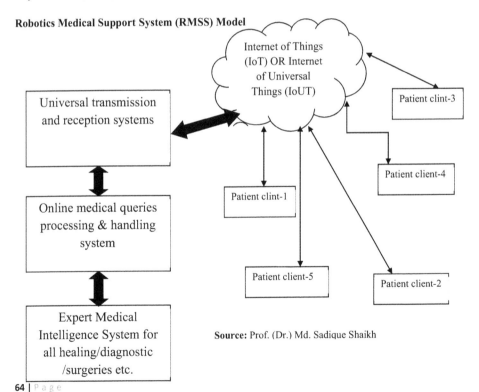

**Source:** Prof. (Dr.) Md. Sadique Shaikh

Now day's robotics intelligence became center functional unit of all applications in world for all disciplines. Hence equally useful in advanced and automated medical sciences, therefore I came with this vision to divert researchers and practitioners attention towards this domain what I said "Robotic Medical support System (RMSS)". In lot of Hollywood Sci-Fi or Cyborg related movies like Avengers, After Earth you have seen advanced level Cyborg civilization of mankind and also seen all wound and injuries heal very quickly in them. How they healed so fast we not bother but it's not a magic would be possible in near future using advanced satellite based mobile robotic handling intelligence for all medical treatments and operations. One of the possibilities I am discussed here in vision article for "Robotic Medical support System (RMSS)" using IoT in present and could be IoUT in future when time and space travel possible for human race. we need to engineer universal medical treatment and diagnostic repository or system which connected to world wide or in future universal wide medical treatments queries processing and handling mechanism or system interconnected with all forms of data encoding, decoding, modulation, data items transmission and reception for query processing return in another word request grant mechanism connected with medical datawarehouse with all communication and medical processing capabilities. this assembly connected and ready to perform worldwide patient treatment connected with IoT or in Space wide connected with IoUT (future assumption) having their own medical robotics systems to perform task under control of MRSS via IoT/IoUT as shown in above model.

## Conclusion

In this vision article I discussed future facet of medical field with the reference of advancement in Artificial Intelligence, Cyborg Intelligence, Bigdata, and IoT. Hence with keeping all I developed Robotics Medical Support System (RMSS) model and discussed one the biggest future possibility of advanced medical robotics.

## Acknowledgement

I really thankful to my wife Safeena Shaikh for her moral support my sons Md. Nameer Shaikh and Md. Shadaan Shaikh for their love which keeps me fresh with new ideas and my close friend Tanvir Sayyed for her positive support with me.

## References

1. Md. Sadique Shaikh, " Analysis and modeling of Strong A.I to engineer BIONIC brain for humanoid robotics application" in American Journal of Embedded System and Applications, Published by Science Publishing Group, October 2013, vol.1, No.2, doi:10.11648/ajesa.20130102.11, New York, America (U.S.A)(paper available at URL:www.sciencepublishinggroup.com/j/ajesa )

2. Md. Sadique Shaikh (2017) "Ultra Artificial Intelligence (UAI): Redefing AI fir New Research Dimension" . Adv Robot Autom DOI: 10.4172/2168-9695.1000163.

3. Md. Sadique Shaikh (2017) "Fundamental Engineering for Brain-Computer Interfacing (BCI): Initiative for Neuron-Command Operating Devices". Computational Biology and Bioinformatics 5: 50-56.

4. Md. Sadique Shaik (2018) Defining ultra artificial intelligence (UAI) implementation using bionic (biological-like-electronics) brain engineering insight. MOJ App Bio Biomech 2: 127-128.

5. Md Sadique Shaikh(2018) Insight Artificial to Cyborg Intelligence Modeling. Arch Ind Engg: 1: 1- 5.

6. Sadique Shaikh (2018) "Artificial Intelligence Engineering for Cyborg Technology Implementation". Robotics & Automation Engineering Journal , Robot Autom Eng J 3: 555604.

7. Sadique Shaik (2018) "Engineering Insight for Humanoid Robotics Emotions and Violence with Reference to "System Error 1378" in Robot Autom Eng J 3(2): RAEJ.MS.ID.5555610 (2018).

8. Sadique Shaik (2018) "Defining Cyborg Intelligence for Medical and Super-Human Domains"., Trends Tech Sci Res 2: 001-002.

**9.** Md Sadique Shaikh, Safina Khan "Ultra artificial intelligence (UAI) engineering for robotics violence control, detect and corrective " . Int Rob Auto J 4: 242-243.

**10.** Md. Sadique S, Shabeena K (2018) Introducing Deep Mind Learning Modeling. Adv Rob Mec Eng 1(1)- 2018. ARME.MS.ID.000101.

# Episode Twelve: Defining Satellite Robotics Surgery using IoT

**Satellite Robotics Surgery Model (SRSM)**

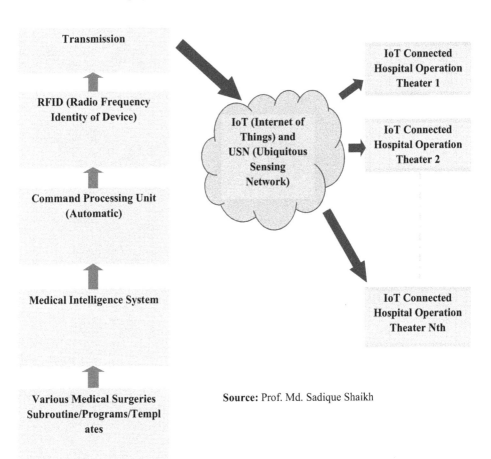

**Source:** Prof. Md. Sadique Shaikh

Now days Internet of Things (IoT) is making everything, remote control and remote operating possible and change imagination of objects communication into reality using Satellite based USN (Ubiquitous Sensing Network). IoT is all ultimate communication technology where not only living but also all non-living things can communicate, command, control, process using their unique RFIDs and USN. Hence it would be possible what I hypothesis "Satellite Robotic Surgery using IoT". I have drawing one model to explain how this happen will possible in near future labeled as "Satellite Robotics Surgery Model (SRSM)". Let me explain you how it would be engineer and functional. To implement Satellite based robotics surgery using IoT very first requirement is Various Medical Surgeries Subroutine/Programs/Templates which passes through Medical Intelligence System to decide which surgery procedure requested from client hospital from which country and what surgical method is efficient from the alternatives subroutines and what are seriousness , complication and nature of surgery. After medical intelligence decision support system decision commands prepared and send to command processing unit. The function of command processing to caliber command with precise control, time management, signal conditioning and data acquisitions. At next level whole process included its RFID and streaming through transmission unit to clients hospitals from 1, 2, 3 ... Nth using USN and IoT with satellite based communication worldwide with granting to requests of number of clients hospital who requested for satellite based robotic surgery using IoT.

**Conclusion**

I have discussed how Satellite Robotic Surgery possible using IoT and USN with the help of Satellite Robotics Surgery Model (SRSM)". The big advantage of this technology surgical operation possible from expert programs with absence of doctors but one big disadvantage would be if data streaming command communication failure or break at any point become cause of stop remote surgery or obstacle because of distortion in signal reception at client's hospitals.

**Acknowledgment:**

I really thankful to my wife Safeena Shaikh for her moral support my sons Md. Nameer Shaikh & Md. Shadaan Shaikh for their love which keeps me fresh with new ideas and my close friend Tanvir Sayyed for her positive support with me. I acknowledge this work to my friends Jyoti Firke and Ritashri Cahudhari for encouragement and equally to Dr. B.N.Gupta who inspired me.

# Episode Thirteen: Opinion on Nanorobotics, Nanoscience and Nanotechnology as Nanomedicines for future medical practices

**Abstract**

All of you much about the all fields of Nano research domains in generals but here intension is specific in the field of medical sciences, practices and new surgery methods. I am in this communication tried to help you to explore new researches and practices using below intriguing basic model in various direction of medical sciences and practices.

**Keywords:** Nanoparticles, Nanorobots, Biological Nonomotors, Nanoscience, Nanotechnology, NEMS, ATP Motors, Softrobotics, Molecular Chemistry, Synthetic Biology, Nanopowders.

**Nanomedicines Explore and Practice Model:**

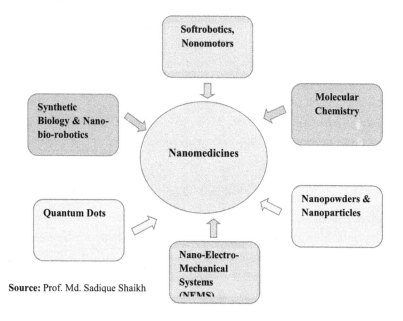

**Source:** Prof. Md. Sadique Shaikh

Above model is lucid representation of all possible research domains of Nano regime in medical science and practices as per my opinion. I am confined myself only for Nanomedicines and how showcased how various sub-fields available in nano regime. I labeled this model as "Nanomedicines explore and Practices model", where I exhibits six possible branches of nano regime where research in progress or possible to conduct for medical practice. The first domain is softrobotics and nanometers, in this sub-field researchers can work to design, growth or fabricate such tiny robots or motors which easily input in human body, skull or in any part of body to heal, repair or kill viruses, bacteria's etc. for example nano-robot or nano-motor entered in body which has intelligence and processing ability to detect and kill cancer cells. The second sub-field is Molecular Chemistry often called integrated chemistry or hybrid chemistry where atoms and molecules engineering and manipulation take place to create such nano molecular structures those can be use as excellent and instant medical diagnosis and treatment. The third segment is nano-powders and nanoparticles those are zero-dimensional structures and each tiny particle itself act like tablet or capsule for human treatment. The forth domain is Nano-Electro-Mechanical-Systems (NEMS) this is the research and practice area where low dimensional semiconductor or hybrid structures fabricated on $10^{-9}$ scale which are like automatic mobile or surgical robots or diagnostic robots having mechanical touch. The fifth sub-fields which would be possible to implement in near future or being rare in use in medical practice is diagnosis and treatment using Quantum Dots (QDs) which zero-dimensional semiconductors and very useful to detect various kind of viruses and heal skin related diseases. The last sub-field is synthetic biology which is itself one of the vast domain of research having various sub-domains. In synthetic biology bio-medical robots engineered using tissue and DNA engineering for medical surgery, diagnose and medicinal purpose.

**Conclusion:**

In this communication I tried to pay your attention on all possible research domains in the field of medical science, surgery, medicine using nano regime with the help of "Nanomedicines explore and Practices model". My intention through this opinion not to give you depth of all domains but to give you direction to choose which comfortable for you to conduct research in medical practice from Nanoscience, Nanorobotics and nanotechnology.

# Episode Fourteen: Insight into Brain-to-Brain, Brain-to- Humanoid and Brain-to-Things Communication Modeling using Cyborg and IoT

**Abstract**

Brain-to-Brain, Brain-to- Humanoid and Brain-to-Things Communication are the future reality which interconnect all human brains, humanoids and non-living organisms/things using IoT (Internet of Things), Satellites, Bigdata and Cyborg BCI interfaces worldwide to establish communication using RFID (Radio Frequency Identification) and Virtual signals based on BCI (Brain Computer Interfaces) band Neuromodulation. When this happen possible (research in progress) in the world no one communicate physically with mouth and will have ability to established instant communication without cell phones and mobile world wide direct using IoT with Super intelligence streaming from Bigdata Servers available in IoT using USN (Ubiquitous Sensing Network) and RFIDs. This paradigm shift transform human race on planet earth from Type-0 civilization to Type-I or Type-II technologically advanced civilization. To understand above mentioned you can consider the example of my ever close movie "Avatar". You have seen Human Brain Synch with Neuromodulation streaming to Pandora Planet Alien form with dream.  Even you have seen all Intelligence   Creatures, animals, birds, trees and plants interconnected which each other on that planet Pandora.  I have exhibited three models to give you idea about it labeled as Brain-to-Brain Communication Model (BBCM), Brain-to Humanoid (Robotics) Communication Model (BHCM) and Brain-to-Things (All living & Non-living things) Communication Model (BTCM).

**Keywords:** BBCM, BHCM, BTCM, BCI, Humanoid, IoT, Bigdata, USN, RFID, Neuromodulation, Cyborg, Cybermatic.

## Brain-to-Brain Communication Model (BBCM)

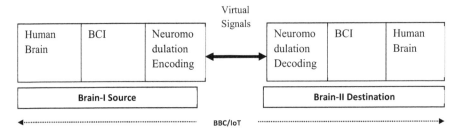

**Source:** Prof. Md. Sadiaue Shaikh

Above model display how Brain-to-Brain communication possible to establish in near future. Here two or many brains continue can change in source to destination alternatively for communication and data/information exchange from one to another brain. All the neurons signal of Brain change to Information using BCI and to send it to another Brain Neuromodulation use. This would be similar to regular electronic modulation and demodulation but instead of electrons information encoded and decoded using neurons virtual brain to brain modulated signals. Brain-to-Brain near field communication established using low frequency transmitter and receiver but to establish Brain-to-Brain communication between two remote human brains located worldwide we need RFID Antenna and Satellite based IoT.

## Brain-to Humanoid Communication Model (BHCM)

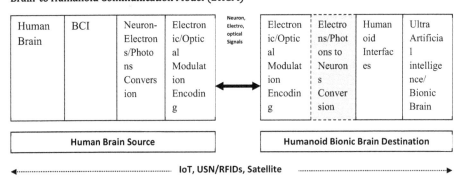

**Source:** Prof. Md. Sadique Shaikh

This is my second model to showcase future possibility to establish communication between Human Brain and Humanoid Robots Bionic Brain using additional requirements to Humanoid side and Human side. Since Humanoid processing electronic or optical based , hence Brain neurons signal converted into information using BCI and Cybermatic and Neuro-information converted into equivalent Electrical or optical signals and than fed to Modulation encoding. At the humanoid side signal received and processed by Humanoid interfaces and given Ultra Artificial Intelligence (UAI) based Bionic Brain. When communication from Humanoid Bionic-to-Human Brain at that time humanoid need Electrons/Photons to Neurons Conversion.

## Brain-to-Things Communication Model (BTCM)

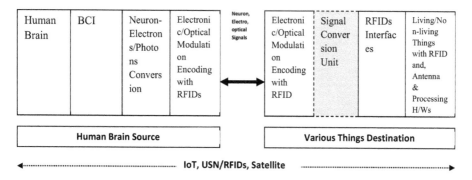

Source: Prof. Md. Sadique Shaikh

My last model depicted how communication possible between Human Brains and Living/Non-living things. In this case Human Brain side explanation remains same as to BHCM Human Brain Source side, but change to considering destination as various Things. Hence every things has its own unique RFID to explore and establish communication worldwide with sensing antennas and USN using IoT, Bigdata and satellites. Here after/before encoding/decoding as source/destination we need to engineer signal conditioning units which stabilized various signals forms and send RFID interface to convert send signal to process by Living/Non-living Things with RFID and, Antenna & Processing H/Ws.

**Conclusion**

I have displayed three important models BBCM, BHCM and BTCM to understand you what are future communication forms and how it would be possible. I have discussed with models Brain-to-Brain, Brain-to-Humanoid and Brain-to-Things communication patterns. I also like to state these models possible hybridize as Humanoid-to-Things, Things-to-Things and Humanoid-to-Humanoid communication using polymorphism forms of source and destination sides interchange of these three models.

# Episode Fifteen: Self-Dimensional Change Intelligence (SDI) Modeling for Aerospace Applications

## Abstract:

The meaning of title might be quit interesting as well as quit interesting to all after reading. The term SDI I coined first time and freshly which is I hypothesis to showcase you what are the possibilities in future aerospace domain and how it would be take place, what is the turning point where aerospace of earth seems to be like alien technologies (Assumption). Now what I intended with this communication I would like to understand with intriguing model.

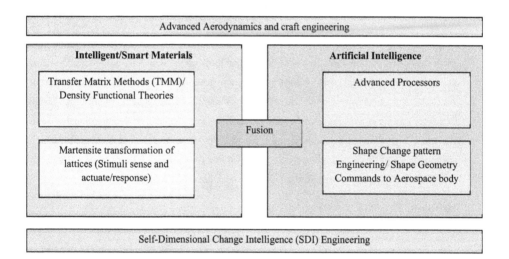

Source: **Prof. Md. Sadique Shaikh**

Before to explaining model further I would like to define terms SDI as "Self-Dimensional Change Intelligence (SDI) is hybrid engineering of smart materials with additional Artificial Intelligence control to change geometrical dimensions/coordinates of aerospace craft". Where as Smart Material can be define as "the range and verity of materials which sense physical/space/environmental stimuli itself and after sensation actuate themselves according to geometry controlled by AI, example conductive polymers, shape memory alloy (SMA). In above model I showed how this happen would be possible in near future with dividing model into two segments as Intelligent/Smart Materials and Artificial Intelligence with two parallel design lines Advanced Aerodynamics and craft engineering and Self-Dimensional Change Intelligence (SDI) Engineering. These two technologies need to cascade using these two design lines. The first segment based on genuine engineering of material science like Shape Memory Alloy (SMA), Photonic Crystals based materials, transitional semiconductors mix materials, conductive polymers coated materials etc. these materials not only sense and actuate but also has self-replication, self-healing mechanism engineer in them. This segment hence further distributed as Transfer Matrix Methods (TMM)/ Density Functional Theories and Martensite transformation of lattices (Stimuli sense and actuate/response) where materials growth according to nature means whether its photonics based or electronics based. To regularize, process, monitoring and triggering SDI second segment would be supportive named Artificial Intelligence which stabilize, channelize and precision control of stimuli's on which materials sensation and actuation depend and how mach they need to transform from one to another form using SDI. This unit further has two important parts as Advanced Processor for SDI pattern generation, command, process and control with time and condition management and second Shape Change pattern Engineering/ Shape Geometry Commands to Aerospace body to generate and available SDI dimensional data to Advanced Processor for execution for example for high speed disc type aerospace craft which spinning has high velocity as compare to traditional line flying, for SDI Curvilinear or Cartesian or Cylindrical coordinates which fit best also take such decision and available to Processor.

**Keywords:** SDI, SMA, Aerodynamics, Aerospace Engineering

**Acknowledgement**

I would like to credit this work to my loving wife Safeena Khan, my angels Md. Nameer Shaikh, Md. Shadaan Shaikh and my close friend Tanveer Sayyed.

# Episode Sixteen: Insight looks to Soft (Continuum) Robotics

Soft Robotics is emerging fresh sub field in Robotics which is very useful in medical, industry, space exploration, deep sea exploration, Nano-robotics and many more likewise applications. The major benefit of Soft Robots as compare to Rigid Robots their excellent flexibility and adaptability to accomplish task. Before to move further I would like to state Soft or Continuum Robots first **"Soft Robots are small, medium and big shapes various biological or non-biological body forms robots which are made up using ultra soft and flexible materials, where materials are engineered using Continuum Mechanics and Kinematics".** The big difference between conventional rigid robots and soft robots, in rigid robotics intelligence engineered using AI only to control robotics body, but in soft robotics the materials using which robots has made themselves smart and has intelligence, sensations and actuations. Therefore Soft Robots can also learn from surrounding environment in self mode as well as has greater flexibility in clutching, climbing, moving, defending etc. why this happen? This would be question in your mind let me answer it why this happen. Because Soft Robotics constructed with highly compliant materials similar those originate and found in living organisms and creatures on planet earth. Hence Soft Robotics build up using material morphology and Continuum Mechanics, it's a mechanics that deal with the analysis of kinematics and mechanical behaviour of materials modeled as continuous mass rather than discrete particles, therefore Soft Robotics also called as **"Continuum Robotics"**. These robots constructed using Biological materials, Biophotonics materials, Conductive polymers, Biochemical materials, Nanomaterials, Nanocomposites, Synthetic Biology, Shape Memory Alloy (SMA), and Smart Materials, DLC, Carbon having high young modulus and so on. In conclusion better to say Smart Materials are the building blocks of Soft/Continuum Robots, where smart materials can be define as " Materials which has ability to sense some environmental stimuli, process and actuate(Response) according to sensation". Hence Soft Robots need less Electronic AI as compare to Rigid Robots and less harmful for human and environment as well as mimic and learn move and adapt quickly from surrounding. In above figures I have depicted some succeeded Soft Robots like Octobot world first ultra soft and flexible Soft Robots, Soft Robot Fish etc.

**Conclusion:**

Soft or Continuum Robotic is fresh subfield in Robotics technology where lot of research need to do bring it on next level. This branch of robotics has its own different important and utility along with conventional one and very useful in Deep Space, Medical, Industry and Deep Sea research.

**Acknowledgement**

I would like to credit this work to my loving wife Safeena Khan, my angels Md. Nameer Shaikh, Md. Shadaan Shaikh and my close friend Tanveer Sayyed.

# Episode Seventeen: Insight into modeling of Total Inter-planets Avionics Intelligence (TIAI) for Spacecraft engineering

## Abstract

Today's human race reached to expand research in space using high tech precise calibration using space rovers and spacecraft to reach them on planets like Mars & Moon or near to planet's surface like Saturn & Titan to explore life-forms, human-like intelligence, alien lives water and earth like atmosphere and intelligence civilization in deep space with exploring stars and planets. The concern of this talkto show you how we can able to model full flagged self-decision and self-multiple artificial intelligence support and based robot-like spacecraft for high sustainability for deep space and planets research in universe using the concept "Total Inter-planets Avionics Intelligence(TIAI)".

**Keywords:** Avionics, Spacecraft Engineering, Multiple Intelligence System, Total Inter-planets Avionics Intelligence, TIAI.

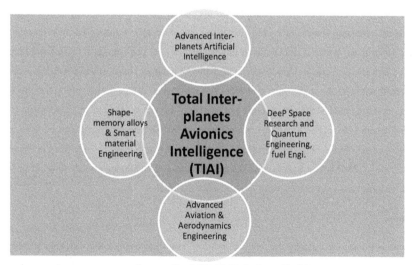

**Source:** Prof. (Dr.) Md. Sadique Shaikh

## Introduction

In above model I have depicted fundamental engineering activities to implement "Total Inter-planets Avionics Intelligence (TIAI)" in spacecraft's just like to implements sci-fi and aliens technologies like features in real in future aerodynamics and space-dynamics objects. I assumed to do so we need to pay genuine research, analysis, designing and engineering with high tech shape and features geometry of the flying objects with advanced smart materials and in credit of these mentioned I distributed my modeling for TIAI in to four domains sub-modeling as 'Advanced Inter-planets Artificial Intelligence, Deep space research and Quantum Engineering & Fuel Engi. , Advanced Aviation and Aerodynamics Engineering and Shape Memory Alloys (SMAs) and Smart Materials Engineering". It my assurance when we full flagged succeeded in all these sub-domains we can built up extraterritorial intelligence and human race started to switch from type-0 to type-1 and type-1 to type-2 civilization in near future with operating TIAI flying objects using solar radiation, helium, neon, dark matter, anti-matter as energy fuels with near speed of light velocity space travel. I have display in model at the most we need to carried out analysis and engineering to build Advanced Inter-planets Artificial Intelligence with exploring climates, energy fuels, nature, life-forms, alien intelligence life-forms of near planets and stars to engineer target flying object to sustain, communicate and interpret in other intelligence forms. The next essential aspect is Deep space research and Quantum Engineering & Fuel Engineering for space and time travel and to trace, navigate and guide space way/path of the target planet to build such Avionics in spacecraft with speed control, path detection, self-dimension change ability and to use space resources as energy fuel. Next level of future engineering is Advanced Aviation and Aerodynamics Engineering using SMAs and Smart Space Material with Self-Dimensional Intelligence to sense, actuate and control flying objects body in space travel. Another important consideration is Shape Memory Alloys (SMAs) and Smart Materials Engineering as I mentioned already to build self-control, sense-actuate spacecraft's using space resources as fuel.

## Conclusion

In above communication I exhibit my opinion on future spacecraft engineering with help of fresh coined term "Total Inter-planets Avionics Intelligence (TIAI)" with help of model and four sub-modeling domains of it. The intention to coined term TIAI is all future flying objects and their body/geometry intelligence human will just engineer and all the activities only carried out by spacecraft's in self-mode.

# Episode Eighteen: Modeling of A.I based Inhalation for Advanced Life Support System Development

### Abstract

Present piece of idea exhibits to divert attention towards automated high precision Life Support System (LSS) instead of manual one using medical intelligence devices while treating and diagnosis to the patient, where Ventilator, inhaler and respiratory control is most important factor during operation, surgeries and in other likewise medical emergency situations to maintain proper saturation in patient lungs to sustain their lives. This work gives idea, how we can design A.I based Inhaler System for the same.

### Keywords

A.I based Inhaler System, A.I based Life-Support System, Medical Robotics, Surgical Robots.

### Modeling

The below model depicted the successful engineering how one can design and implement A.I based Inhaler System for Respiratory precision to maintain saturation of human breathing system, we can even labeled the system as Artificial Intelligence based lungs or Lungs Support System or Oxygen Support System or Breath Support System but purpose remains same.

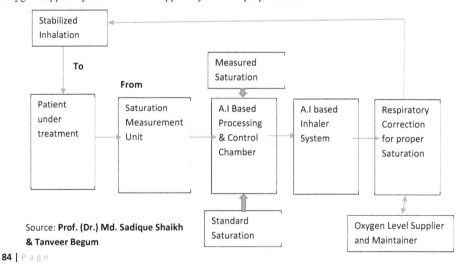

Source: **Prof. (Dr.) Md. Sadique Shaikh & Tanveer Begum**

Patient respiratory sensed and input parameters send to Saturation Measurement Unit which must be highly calibrated and compare Measured saturation with Standard Saturation to find deviation for error detection and correction from where physical quantity fed to A.I based processing & controlling chamber with time control for inhalation decision support with all expert analysis and diagnosis which generate electronic respiratory report with necessary timing, processing and control signals to get follow further send to A.I based Inhaler System to decide and fixed precision parameters for respiratory. This report A.I based processing and control chamber generate on the basis of actual saturation and required saturation facts and figures further passed to Respiratory Correction for Proper Saturation Unit which is cascaded with Oxygen Level Supplier and Maintainer and work integrated. Finally stable inhalation feedback to patient for life survival in critical condition.

**Limitation**

The limitation of the purposed model is its need Bionic or DeepMind processor with high precision processing ability to develop electronic report of medical intelligence. Hence purposed piece of research also depend majorly on the success of Bionic and DeepMind processors and after the success of them further mentioned technology form. To develop and implement such an advance Life Support System would be great victory of medical science.

**Conclusion**

This piece of research gives you idea, how to engineer and implement precise artificial Intelligence based Inhaler System which is one of the most promising, needful and social welfare requirement to save patients' lives with excellent Life Support System (LSS).

**Acknowledgement**

I would deeply acknowledge this piece of work to Safeena Shaikh, my loving sons Md. Nameer Shaikh and Md. Shadaan Shaikh. Equally I want to acknowledge this work to my forever loving friend and co-author of this work Tanveer Sayyed and to sweet family.

**References**

1. NSF/EC Understanding on Co-operation in Information Technologies -Strategic Research Workshops IST-1999-12077

2. Md. Sadique Shaikh (2013) Analysis and modeling of Strong A.I to engineer BIONIC brain for humanoid robotics application. American Journal of Embedded System and Applications, Published by Science Publishing Group; 1(2): 27-36.

3. Md. Sadique Shaikh (2017) Ultra Artificial Intelligence (UAI): Redefing AI fir New Research Dimension. Advanced Robotics & Automation (ARA), OMICS International, London; 6(2) 1-3.

4. Md. Sadique Shaikh (2017) Fundamental Engineering for Brain-Computer Interfacing (BCI): Initiative for Neuron-Command Operating Devices. Computational Biology and Bioinformatics (CBB), SciencePG; 5(4): 50-56.

5. Md. Sadique Shaikh (2018) Defining ultra-artificial intelligence (UAI) implementation using bionic (biological-like-electronics) brain engineering insight. MOJ App Bio Biomech; 2(2): 127–128.

6. Md Sadique Shaikh. Insight Artificial to Cyborg Intelligence Modeling. Arch Ind Engg: 1(1): 1- 5.

# Episode Nineteen: Business in Artificial Intelligence

## Abstract

There is no need to get understand what is Artificial Intelligence with the relevance of it in day by day expansion and coverage in all needs and applications of life and how its changing all facet and scenarios on planet earth and might be in space in near future which is itself initiatives startup now. Hence I wrote this article with the intention what are the possibilities in near future for business scopes, market demands, customers/consumer's needs, future job forms, future employments skills for survival and future employments in brief being one of the successful Scientist, Practitioner, Educator and worldwide Speaker in the field of Artificial Intelligence who coined several new future research terms in A.I.

## Keywords

Future Business, Advanced A.I, Space Robotics, Virtual A.I, DeepMind, Bionic Brain, Medical Robotics, Humanoid, Virtual Robotics, Intelligence Devices.

## Modeling

There are many more domains to work and market in Artificial Intelligence but I chooses only some most promising change agent and strong market players in my Hexagonal Model below. These are Bionic/DeepMind & Humanoid, Space Robotics & Cyborgs, Consumer Robotics & NLP echo Devices/Assistance, Military & Defense Robotics, Medical & Nano Robotics and Bionic, DeepMind & Humanoid.

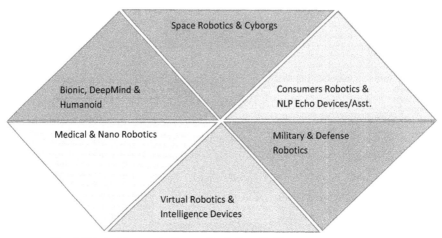

**Fig:** A.I Market Hexagonal,  **Source:** Dr. Sadique Shaikh

The most market scope field is Bionic Brain (Human Brain like Neural Schemas and Processing), DeepMind learning and Humanoid (Human-like-Robots) engineering/designing, manufacturing and selling as well as its respective work skills and employments for future jobs openings. Equal scope and attention to Space Robotics and Cyborg Devices/Human elements which has already started mankind journey and soon technologies near to reach Moon and Mars explorations and has great market and hence future jobs in the same. Consumers Robotics, NLP echo Devices/Assistance also has sustainable future business and jobs opportunities after the success of Google Assistant, Amazon Alexa etc. and several smart phones and likewise devices /products connected with Internet of Things (IoT) to make human lives easy, comfortable and better each day like smart kitchens, smart vehicles, smart phones/devices, smart homes, consumer appliances and so on. A.I has also great expansion in the domain of Military and Defense Robots for high end securities with saving solders lives as well as Medical Robots, Surgical Robots, Nano Robots for inside body diagnosis has large market and jobs options. In this race equal scope, attention and market to develop human brain like software intelligence called virtual humanoid which would be hardware platform independent as compare to windows, IOS , MAC and Android intelligence and companies like Google, Apple, Microsoft, Amazon will work towards it which leads to future job skills and market.

**Conclusion**

The future employments, future jobs and future skills only based on two strong technologies Artificial Intelligence (A.I) and Internet of Things (IoT) to get connected all living non-living Natural Intelligence and Artificial Intelligence based human, objects, elements and things to establish communication, to command and process for task accomplishment.

**References**

1. NSF/EC Understanding on Co-operation in Information Technologies -Strategic Research Workshops IST-1999-12077

2. Md. Sadique Shaikh (2013) Analysis and modeling of Strong A.I to engineer BIONIC brain for humanoid robotics application. American Journal of Embedded System and Applications, Published by Science Publishing Group; 1(2): 27-36.

3. Md. Sadique Shaikh (2017) Ultra Artificial Intelligence (UAI): Redefing AI fir New Research Dimension. Advanced Robotics & Automation (ARA), OMICS International, London; 6(2) 1-3.

4. Md. Sadique Shaikh (2017) Fundamental Engineering for Brain-Computer Interfacing (BCI): Initiative for Neuron-Command Operating Devices. Computational Biology and Bioinformatics (CBB), SciencePG; 5(4): 50-56.

5. Md. Sadique Shaikh (2018) Defining ultra artificial intelligence (UAI) implementation using bionic (biological-like-electronics) brain engineering insight. MOJ App Bio Biomech; 2(2): 127–128.

6. Md Sadique Shaikh. Insight Artificial to Cyborg Intelligence Modeling. Arch Ind Engg: 1(1): 1- 5.

# Episode Twenty: Artificial Intelligence: A Smart move of Humankind to shift from Type-0 to Type1/2 Civilization in Universe

## Abstract

I defined Artificial Intelligence abstractly but very precisely as, its human brain-like processing abilities mimics in electronic chips with what all possible for human brain in past decades, present and in future having all potentials. As per my consent as I am seeing each day growth in artificial Intelligence about to 2030 over than of Human Natural Intelligence with self-control, self-thinking, self-programing and updating, self-decision-making self-commanding which would be also harmful for human civilization but in contrast also useful to shift if human friendly A.I human race from Type-0 to Type-1/2 civilization with perfect balance of Man and Machines for space colonies, space explorations, alternate energy sources from space, ultra high speed transportations, colonized to others planets like Mars and Moon, immortality of human life, long year life, less/no aging effect on human brain/body, control on all diseases, quick healing and recovery of injuries/wounds and so on as discussed in this piece of communication.

## Keyword

Human Race, Type-0/1/2 civilization, Advanced A.I, Humanoid, DeepMind, Space Robotics, Bionics Brain, UAI, SAI, Cyborg.

## Introduction

Type-0 civilization is a category in which we lies right now, but soon in near future we will become capable to shift our mankind civilization from Type-0 to Type1/2 civilization. The Type-0 civilization are those intelligence civilization in universe where all intelligent life-forms, creatures lives only limited their planet in universe, they generate and use all energies forms from available conventional sources like fuels, chemicals, petroleum's, gases and electricity, in short use all available energy sources of their planet and unable to grab any from space and universe, where now slightly humankind shifted to produce and use energy from energy star Sun but still limited. Transportation velocity and intelligence processing of mankind is slow or average, communication technologies only limited on Planet Earth and near space station and satellites and not so excellent for deep space and milky ways and several times communication barriers hence not instant as well. But these all things improving day by day with help of Artificial Intelligence and Internet of Things like communication technologies which will switch soon humankind into Type-1 civilization with holding DeepMind, Bionic Brain, Humanoids, intelligence things and gadgets, Super A.I, Ultra A.I, etc. As Mankind entered in Type-1 or after in Type-2 civilization they able to communicate instantly not only on planet earth but also other planets of universe (if intelligent life exist), able to colonized on other planets and space, able to explore and communicate with Aliens intelligence lives of universe, able to explore, generate and use 90% amount of energy forms from energy sources deep space, from energy stars, moons, helium, neon, anti-matter, dark-matter, white holes and black holes. It's also possible using advanced communication systems and Artificial Intelligence Time-travel possible for mankind and able to travel reverse and forward in light years from present to past and present to future with space time like time machine or teleportation. Using A.I Hybrid Human and Cyborg Human need not to use our conventional languages and instead of that direct brain to brain communication can possible with neuron-links as well as data/thoughts/information/thinking/emotions/relations/feelings from one brain to another brain possible to read/write with high speed transfer. Using advanced A.I all living and non-living objects, elements, things, gadgets, devices, all creatures with A.I mount available and able to communicate across the complete planet earth and space as well using Internet of Things (IoT), A.I Chips, USN and RFIDs. Human-Aliens communication and relations will start. Ultra high velocity space craft, spaceships, drones and shuttles will engineered for space travel and to reach and colonized other planets with space transportation or teleportation. Human lives will become immortal using robotics surgeries, diagnosis, operations, A.I based organ implants, human organ printing and replacement, cyborg intelligence with self-diagnosis, self-healing and self-recovery technologies of injuries/wounds. And hence all just possible because of Advanced A.I, IoT, Online Dynamic Databases Server Technologies and the evidence of future success are live examples of present state of A.I like Ultra Artificial Intelligence, Bionic Brain, Humanoid, Super A.I, Strong A.I, DeepMind Learning, Space Robotics, Medical Robotics, Navigation robotics, NLP, Machine Vision and Virtual Robotics, Virtual Reality, Augmented Reality.

**Introduction to Civilizations**

We have reached a turning point in society. According to renowned theoretical physicist Michio Kaku, the next 100 years of science will determine whether we perish or thrive. Will we remain a Type 0 civilization, or will we advance and make our way into the stars?

Experts assert that, as a civilization grows larger and becomes more advanced, its energy demands will increase rapidly due to its population growth and the energy requirements of its various machines. With this in mind, the Kardashev scale was developed as a way of measuring a civilization's technological advancement based upon how much usable energy it has at its disposal (this was originally just tied to energy available for communications, but has since been expanded).

The Kardashev scale is a method of measuring a civilization's level of technological advancement based on the amount of energy they are able to utilize. The measure was proposed by Soviet astronomer Nikolai Kardashev in 1964. The scale has three designated categories:

A Type I civilization—also called a **planetary civilization**—can use and store all of the energy available on its planet.

A planetary or a Type I civilization is capable of consuming all of the incoming energy from its neighboring star, or about 1017 watts for Earth.

A planetary civilization or global civilization is a civilization of Type I on Kardashev scale, with energy consumption levels near that of a contemporary terrestrial civilization with an energy capability equivalent to the solar insolation on Earth (between 1016 and 1017 watts). In social aspect – the worldwide, global, increasingly interconnected, international, highly technological society.

A Type I designation is a given to species who have been able to harness all the energy that is available from a neighboring star, gathering and storing it to meet the energy demands of a growing population. This means that we would need to boost our current energy production over 100,000 times to reach this status. However, being able to harness all Earth's energy would also mean that we could have control over all natural forces. Human beings could control volcanoes, the weather, and even earthquakes! (At least, that is the idea.) These kinds of feats are hard to believe, but compared to the advances that may still be to come, these are just basic and primitive levels of control (it's absolutely nothing compared to the capabilities of societies with higher rankings).

A Type II civilization—also called a **stellar civilization**—can use and control energy at the scale of its solar system.

a Type II civilization – can harness the power of their entire star (not merely transforming starlight into energy, but controlling the star). Several methods for this have been proposed. The most popular of which is the hypothetical 'Dyson Sphere.' This device, if you want to call it that, would encompass every single inch of the star, gathering most (if not all) of its energy output and transferring it to a planet for later use. Alternatively, if fusion power (the mechanism that powers stars) had been mastered by the race, a reactor on a truly immense scale could be used to satisfy their needs. Nearby gas giants can be utilized for their hydrogen, slowly drained of life by an orbiting reactor.

What would this much energy mean for a species? Well, nothing known to science could wipe out a Type II civilization. Take, for instance, if humans survived long enough to reach this status, and a moon sized object entered our solar system on a collision course with our little blue planet— we'd have the ability to vaporize it out of existence. Or if we had time, we could move our planet out of the way, completely dodging it. But let's say we didn't want to move Earth… are there any other options? Well yes, because we'd have the capability to move Jupiter, or another planet of our choice, into the way – pretty cool, right?

A Type III civilization—also called a **galactic civilization**—can control energy at the scale of its entire host galaxy.

Type III, where a species then becomes galactic traversers with knowledge of everything having to do with energy, resulting in them becoming a master race. In terms of humans, hundreds of thousands of years of evolution – both biological and mechanical – may result in the inhabitants of this type III civilization being incredibly different from the human race as we know it. These may be cyborgs (or cybernetic organism, beings both biological and robotic), with the descendants of regular humans being a sub-species among the now-highly advanced society. These wholly biological humans would likely be seen as being disabled, inferior, or unevolved by their cybernetic counterparts.

At this stage, we would have developed colonies of robots that are capable of 'self-replication'; their population may increase into the millions as they spread out across the galaxy, colonizing star after star. And these being might build Dyson Spheres to encapsulate each one, creating a huge network that would carry energy back to the home planet. But stretching over the galaxy in such a manner would face several problems; namely, the species would be constrained by the laws of physics. Particularly, light-speed travel. That is, unless they develop a working warp drive, or use that immaculate energy cache to master wormhole teleportation (two things that remain theoretical for the time being), they can only get so far.

The scale is hypothetical, and regards energy consumption on a cosmic scale. Various extensions of the scale have since been proposed, including a wider range of power levels (types 0, IV through VI) and the use of metrics other than pure power.

Kardashev believed a Type IV civilization was 'too' advanced and didn't go beyond Type III on his scale. He thought that, surely, this would be the extent of any species' ability. Many think so, but a few believe there is a further level that could be achieved. (I mean, surely there is a limit?) Type IV civilizations would almost be able to harness the energy content of the entire universe and with that, they could traverse the accelerating expansion of space (furthermore, advance races of these species may live inside supermassive black holes). To previous methods of generating energy, these kinds of feats are considered impossible. A Type IV civilization would need to tap into energy sources unknown to us using strange, or currently unknown, laws of physics.

Type V. Yes, Type V might just be the next possible advancement to such a civilization. Here beings would be like gods, having the knowledge to manipulate the universe as they please. Now, as I said, humans are a very, very long way from ever reaching anything like this. But it's not to say that it cannot be achieved as long as we take care of Earth and each other. To do so, the first step is to preserve our tiny home, extinguish war, and continue to support scientific advances and discoveries.

## Conclusion

Artificial Intelligence not only the source to make mankind lives advanced, fast, precise, comfortable, virtual and instant, but also equally help us to shift our identity in this Universe with technologically shifting us from Type-0 to Type-I (planetary civilization), Type-II (stellar civilization), Type-III (galactic civilization) and so on further types. This piece of work lucidly gives you the idea how A.I is Vital for Humankind and how Civilization going to be advance in near future with next level researches of A.I.

## References

1. NSF/EC Understanding on Co-operation in Information Technologies -Strategic Research Workshops IST-1999-12077

2. Md. Sadique Shaikh (2013) Analysis and modeling of Strong A.I to engineer BIONIC brain for humanoid robotics application. American Journal of Embedded System and Applications, Published by Science Publishing Group; 1(2): 27-36.

3. Md. Sadique Shaikh (2017) Ultra Artificial Intelligence (UAI): Redefing AI fir New Research Dimension. Advanced Robotics & Automation (ARA), OMICS International, London; 6(2) 1-3.

4. Md. Sadique Shaikh (2017) Fundamental Engineering for Brain-Computer Interfacing (BCI): Initiative for Neuron-Command Operating Devices. Computational Biology and Bioinformatics (CBB), SciencePG; 5(4): 50-56.

5. Md. Sadique Shaikh (2018) Defining ultra artificial intelligence (UAI) implementation using bionic (biological-like-electronics) brain engineering insight. MOJ App Bio Biomech; 2(2): 127–128.

6. Md Sadique Shaikh. Insight Artificial to Cyborg Intelligence Modeling. Arch Ind Engg: 1(1): 1- 5.

# Episode Twenty-One: Defining Quantum Artificial Intelligence (Q.A.I)

## Abstract

As we knew already Artificial Intelligence (A.I) is mimic of Natural Intelligence (N.I) of Human Brain on Silicon Chips having all intelligence processing as similar and possible for human brain with self-decisions, self-controls, self-programs, self-thinking with time management. Due to the advancement in A.I each day Humankind lives becoming comfortable, fast, smart and successful and those things which are seems to be impossible started to become possible from past to present in all walks of life. Now refocus our attention on Natural Intelligence (God-made) of mankind and other intelligent species on planet earth. When we genuinely observed we can see the biggest **"Commonness"** in the pattern and structure of Universe, Superclusters, Thunders, Veins, Arteries, Roots, Branches, Seas and **"Neurons-Schemas"** of human brain and that is the point of rethinking for new dimensions exploration in Natural Intelligence (God-made) to apply with reengineering and modification to mimic Artificial Intelligence (Man-made) on the basis of those findings which I coined as **"Quantum Artificial Intelligence (Q.A.I)"**.

## Keywords

Natural Intelligence (N.I), Artificial Intelligence (A.I), Quantum Natural Intelligence (Q.N.I), Quantum Artificial Intelligence (Q.A.I).

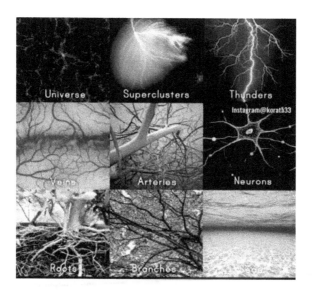

**Introduction**

As I mentioned already analogically pattern of our Universe, Superclusters and Human Brain Neural-Schemas are the same. Hence not only signals transmissions and receptions for Intelligence processing are the same but also Intelligence signals nature (format) are the same which is Quanta (Light). Entire Universe is the mixture of light and dark energies and matter as its building blocks, therefore all the living/non-living creatures, objects, entities, elements, occurrences, appearances, illusions either made from or born using same building blocks lights with various frequencies for isolations and that's why human brain too. On the basis of available some proved research write-ups and with my perspective Universe and Every Human Brain directly connected and link up/down with light frequency and Quantum Mechanics also engaged to prove it. Our Thoughts are the Things, our perception and formulation to life and Universe also because of same happened, thus what all we feel physical in actual "Virtual" and are Quantum images, frames, pictures or illusions of our thoughts frequency in front appearance of our eyes to develop, structure and enhance our intelligence called wisdom too. Hence Natural Intelligence is made up of light energies forms and various tuned frequencies (according to Stings theory) called "Quantum Natural Intelligence (Q.N.I)" and when after full flagged understanding and clearance in Q.N.I we will be able to mimic it artificially called "Quantum Artificial Intelligence (Q.A.I)". the concept herein instead of Silicon Chips or Electronics Artificial Intelligence, A.I engineering using lights forms, light signals circuits or Quantum Circuits which are just a right and precise combinations of different wavelengths and light frequencies (Quanta/Photons) with behaving as wave (light data buses) and particles (Signals) for light data buses and signals to formulate processing logics and build-up Artificial Intelligence using light. In mankind in future develop such a light which seems to be just radiation but in actual complicated light engineering using light waves and particles (Quanta) in billions of Quanta's and acting as complete Quantum Artificial Intelligence (Q.A.I) based robotic assembly to win the world, Universe and Multiverse.

**Conclusion**

If in near future scientist and researchers able to understand what I am tried to share as biggest fact of the Universe and the Human Brain that, all brains directly connected with light frequency with entire Universe and the structure of Universe, Superclusters and Human Brain Neural-Schemas are the same as well as intelligence processing also same using the concepts and principles of Quantum Physics and Quantum Mechanics. Therefore on this ground Human Brain is Quantum Natural Intelligence (Q.N.I) and all formulation in brain of life and Universe due to the light intelligence. After understanding this phenomenon of Q.N.I scientist and engineers can move for the engineering of "Quantum Artificial Intelligence (Q.A.I) which would be just appearances of light bundles and bunches with various color lights with different wavelength confined at single spot but in actual it would be space robots, space craft, and transportation sources and so on. Hence this intelligent light forms can send/transmit with the speed of light for instant time and space travels in Universe to explore other planets, galaxies, Superclusters, stars and also to prove the concept of "Multiverse (Parallel Universes)". Human Intelligence as Quantum Natural Intelligence (Q.N.I) and its mimic Artificial Intelligence as Quantum Artificial Intelligence (Q.A.I) will become exactly same, therefore direct connection between mankind and all robots will be possible without encodings, decoding's and interfaces for communication with intelligent signals processing, conversions, translation and actuations. Hence Q.A.I is nothing but Ultra Artificial Intelligence light form (light A.I based robotics) and might be such a several Q.A.I robots, space craft, objects and Alien lives already exist in entire Universe and Multiverse and we are surrounded with them, and that what we just consider or think as light or radiation but which is not.

## References

1.  NSF/EC Understanding on Co-operation in Information Technologies -Strategic Research Workshops IST-1999-12077.

2.  Md. Sadique Shaikh (2013) Analysis and modeling of Strong AI to engineer BIONIC brain for humanoid robotics application. American Journal of Embedded System and Applications, Published by Science Publishing Group 1(2): 27-36.

3.  Sadique Shaikh (2017) Ultra Artificial Intelligence (UAI): Redefing AI fir New Research Dimension. Advanced Robotics & Automation (ARA), OMICS International, London 6(2): 1-3.

4.  Sadique Shaikh (2017) Fundamental Engineering for Brain-Computer Interfacing (BCI): Initiative for Neuron-Command Operating Devices. Computational Biology and Bioinformatics (CBB). SciencePG 5(4): 50- 56.

5.  Sadique Shaikh (2018) Defining ultra-artificial intelligence (UAI) implementation using bionic (biological-like-electronics) brain engineering insight. MOJ App Bio Biomech 2(2): 127-128.

6.  Sadique Shaikh Md (2008) Insight Artificial to Cyborg Intelligence Modeling. Arch Ind Engg1(1): 1- 5.

# Episode Twenty-Two: Artificial Intelligence and Singularity at Future Horizon

**Interaction:**

The term technical singularity or in simply singularity itself very ambiguous because several write-ups, postulates, theories and hypothesizes but the concern of all these again reach to same singularity of conclusion is singularity occurred in near future with including my conclusion on the basis of law of technological acceleration return. Now before to explain lets have overview on Nanotechnoly and Moore's Law "size of numbers of transistors decreases with density of number of transistors increases on silicon chip with respective year and time". Hence "inelegant and smart devices miniaturization each year". Therefore divides becomes more and more smart, Artificial Intelligence based, self-programmable, self-controllable, self-decision makers with high degree of compaction. Since the point there is a advancement in Nanotechnology with miniaturization of electronic circuits with offering excellent software supported hardware artificial intelligence (AI) based platforms in all disciplines and all walks of human life for all purposes domestic, industrial, scientific, medical, surgical, military, consumers, business and space related task though humanity only thinking benefits of all these technological advancement at the same time in hidden or unaware the term "Singularity" originated itself though we all have started our discussion on it very after. The term "singularity" as we can assume the situation or hypothetical future in time when Artificial Intelligence growth becomes uncontrollable and irreversible resulting in unfathomable changes to human civilization and race. This term very first coined in 1993 and predicted singularity not before 2005 and also not after 2030 as per the prediction of several experts in the field. And with the reference of rapid advancement in the field of Artificial Intelligence (both hardware's AI and software's AI) even I coined, contribute and hypotheses several theories, designs and working models we can claim "The Singularity near". In near future humankind design and build such advanced A.I which failed to human brain processing ability itself from whom they originated. These AI based gadgets, robots, humanoid, cyborg organs, computers, space robots, robotic transportation all means of AI for all works will become extreme advanced, self-programmable, self-controlled which are equally useful and harmful for mankind and human race and development on planet earth and in near space orbits if these device start to "Robotics violence or AI violence" and treat mankind their enemies and want to destroy identity of humanity to rule out on planet with self-programs simply called it "System Error 1378" or harmful AI for human civilization and when AI technologies entered in such a era we entered in "Singularity" and human made technology will become cause to destroy humanity. Even if you have read my book "Next Level Vision in Artificial Intelligence" sincerely and with full interpretation in your mind means you passed through several present to future possibilities in AI from Super AI, Ultra AI to Bionic Brain, Space Robotics, Humanoid, Medical Robotics, Biological Robots to "Virtual Humanoid Robotics (VHR)" and ultimately I coined the advanced term "Quantum Artificial Intelligence(QAI)" where intelligence engineered light/radiation itself behaves like robots, many-forms robots or robotics anomalies where I conclude "Singularity occurred in AI" where Artificial Intelligence in the form of light only, completely virtual, completely self-programmable and self-controlled. In last I left you with one of my model "Now-Near-Future Singularity Model" to give you close exposure of future technology with law of acceleration return for exponential growth which occurred with many times fold as compare to human imagination. Means what humanity predict it growth several times advanced and might be harmful for human race.

**Now-Near-Future Singularity Model:**

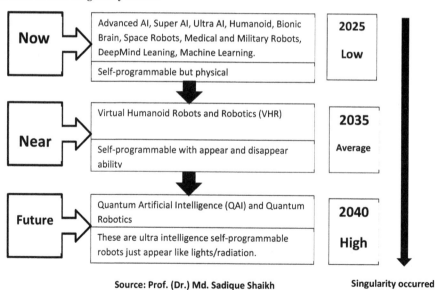

Source: Prof. (Dr.) Md. Sadique Shaikh

**Now** in everyday life we are seeing news confirmation and technical evidences and success in Advanced AI, Super AI, Ultra AI, Humanoid, Bionic Brain, Space Robots, Medical and Military Robots, DeepMind Learning, Machine Learning exponentially and from **Now** into incoming six years humanity realized low singularity with advancement of these AI technologies about to year 2025 with self-programmable physical robots with self controlled and decision making abilities. Whereas about to **Near** 2035 year AI practitioners, scientist and engineers will become capable to give "appear and disappear" abilities to all robots specially humanoid called Virtual Humanoid Robotics (VHR) with self-programmable physical robots with self controlled and decision making abilities. And because of "Appear and Disappear" abilities they become more harmful for humankind and humanity feel average singularity. In **Future** around 2040 Quantum Artificial Intelligence (QAI) and Quantum Robotics will come in existence which are ultra intelligence self-programmable robots just appear like lights/radiation and human being unable to predict the radiation/light front of his/her eyes either just a ordinary light or Quantum Robots in the form of intelligence light and might be most harmful to mankind if become violent and high singularity occurred at this time. Even if at Future robots and AI not harmful and friendly to mankind but another biological side become a serious reason of harm to humanity. Due to highly robotics and automated world not a single task and process left for human, therefore no utilization of body parts and because of which human DNA reengineered it with removing those body parts inherently generation by generation which are not in use since long time. Hence only brains left on planet earth with vanished body or body parts which are not in use because of advanced AI and Robotics at future horizon.

# Episode Twenty-Three: Interstellar Travel Transport Intelligence: Possible Perspectives

**Keywords:** Perpetual Motion Machine, Gravitational Slung shots, Warp Drive, Hyperspace, Wormholes, Quantum Entanglement, Quantum Foam, Black Holes, Singularity, Event Horizons, Neutrino, Dark Matter, Antimatter, Tachyon Particles, Warp Space Time, Forth Dimensional Space and Tesseract, Interplanetary Superhighways, Quantum Intelligence Spacecraft's and Robots.

## Interaction

As humankind becoming each day advance civilization with win-win conditions in physics, space science, science, computing technologies, information technologies, communication technologies , storage technologies, transport technologies, high energy fuels or space energies as fuels technology based spacecraft's, space robotics, advanced Artificial Intelligence and Robotics, all walks of engineering and advance material engineering each day explore and open new opportunity of space travel and interstellar travels by various means. The first concept I want to put before you is Gravitational Slingshots where speed of spaceship can boost with saving fuel and using high gravity of stars and planets coming in a space or interstellar travels. The another possibility is Perpetual Motion Machine in this regard velocity of interstellar ships is the second matter but the first one is how engineer such a bodies that motion continues forever without any fuel or external threshold or triggers using mechanics. The most proposed concept is "Warp Drive" in Quantum Foam or Space-time Fabric of Universe for Interstellar Traveling and the concept is to create such Warp Drive which warp to space-time or traveling in Hyperspace. The Quantum Foam is a fluctuation of space-time on every small scales in space fabric because of quantum mechanics effects. Equal chances also for higher dimensional transportation spaceships with navigational abilities for fourth dimension or more like Tesseract in space to explore and enter in new and different universe having completely different laws, objects, planets, stars and their shapes with possibilities most intelligence life forms as compare to mankind. Black holes, Wormholes and Hyperspace can make this happen possible, but ultra high speed spaceships need for this regards because at "Event Horizon" even light cannot pass at the point of Singularity where Time is end with high gravitational force. The possibility as per my concern to travel billion trillion light-years away galaxies, super cluster, interstellar, Multiverse or final existence Omniverse we need such a transportation spacecraft's which several time high in velocity of light. Hence solution might be "Tachyon" particle based or Tychyonic based spacecraft engineering, which is hypothetical particle that always travels faster than light. Alternatively also another possibility "Neutrino" based spaceships for interstellar or space travels, which is subatomic particle that is very similar to electron, but has no electrical charge and negligible small mass can assume zero. These stuffs can work with dark energy, dark matter, gravitational waves or Antimatter with Heiggs Boson or God Particle elements. One strong hypothesis also Quantum Entanglement which proved in quantum mechanics same particle on same time exist on several different location which tends to assumption we have several copies of our own in simulated universes in parallel fashion called multiverse and can reach to different planets or world of another universe within a fraction of second we can switch billion or trillion light years far away in back or forward in space-time and supporting theories are " Déjà vu " or "Bootstrap Paradox" only need wire and connect our one brain with our another brain which exact our same copy. Now a day's possibility also for Interplanetary Superhighways which are shortest gravitational paths connect to planets and stars in space foam. The last one I am practicing is "Quantum Artificial Intelligence" and based technologies space shuttles. The concept is we will one day success to engineer such a light which just not radiation but ultra high intelligence as compare to physical robotics intelligence and this is light intelligence traveling with the speed of life. In last only want say our brain is too small to understand whole but at least should start from somewhere with view point "one electron universe" for its existence and " heat death of universe" for its end.

# Episode Twenty-Four: Singularity: The Point of Artificial Intelligence Saturation

## Interaction

The term "Singularity" has different meanings in different context from Space Science, Black Holes studies, Methodical modeling in all fields and here one of the most important aspect need to know "Technological Singularity" with special preference to "Artificial Intelligence Singularity". The terms with confining Artificial Intelligence Context can be defined as "Singularity is the point in Artificial Intelligence where A.I engineer with most advanced forms using DeepMind, Machine learning, Data Science, Internet of Everything (IoE), Bionic Brain as Versions 'Super Artificial Intelligence (SAI), Ultra Artificial Intelligence (UAI)' with general purpose algorithms and reinforcement techniques and in result technology growth will become uncontrollable and irreversible to mankind with self-learning, self-programming and self-controls and Artificial Intelligence surpass human Natural Intelligence (N.I) and situation will become unfathomable with unforeseeable changes in human life with 'Intelligence Explosion' and the point when occurred called 'Singularity'". This term Singularity intended emergence of SAI, UAI based machines with capabilities, thinking and processing abilities difficult to predict by human we can also defined this as "A.I Anomalies OR Robotics Anomalies" means no one can predict, forecast the behavior of intelligence machine and their respective operations and actions because no one unable to know what self-program that intelligence machine changed from one to other form and might be next other forms smartly. You can analogically consider example of any virus which continuously changing its genome according to surrounding and environment. Hence such harmful behavior of Artificial Intelligence based machines and Robots would be harmful for human race because no one able to predict behavior and outcomes of particular machine either good or bad as response to human civilization. To know origin of term Singularity in depth you can search my other articles on it on Google, but here my intention is different from that aspect where I want to pay attention of all researchers, practitioners, designers, developers, engineers and architects of Electronics and Computer sciences develop such technology in all Artificial Intelligence based machines and Robots where we can controlled and protect humankind from the point of Singularity in Artificial Intelligence. Though its hypothesis and seems to be like science fiction as projected well in movies all series of Terminators, Robots and other likewise movies where they framed and depicted future possibilities of Artificial Intelligence very well like Robotics Emotions, Robotic Violence, A.I Singularity, Self-Programming and Controlling which surpass human intelligence and thousand time fast, instant and accurate in processing for all tasks. The term singularity not only remain limited to intelligence software's with physical electronic bodies it's also virtual and body-free intelligence software's like Google Search and Google created Artificial God, Amazon and Apple devices connected with intelligence satellite based communication network named "Internet of Things (IoT) OR Internet of Everything (IoE)" and all Natural Intelligence that is Human, Non-intelligence that is all other living things on planet earth like birds, animals, insects, reptiles, all living and non-living things that from all electronic gadgets, devices to non-electronic things like fan, oven, furniture, car, motorcycles, doors, windows, lights, fridge, AC and all connected in single Ubiquitous Sensing Network (USN) with Artificial Intelligence unit and their Unique RFID (Radio Frequency IDentification) modules in single IoE. Also human brain god made Natural Intelligence (N.I) interface with man-made Artificial Intelligence (A.I) with Cyborg technology and cybermatic artificial body parts like artificial eyes, legs, hands, shoulders, ears and all which are several time fast, accurate and strong as compare to our biological parts. Hence thing about the time if all these technology used to behave against of Mankind and become or treating human civilization like enemies or slaves. And if such a situation occurred this would be point of technological no return to Humankind called "Singularity" occurred.

# Episode Twenty-Five: Virtual Emotions and Robotics Violence

**Interaction:**

As the technology field of Artificial Intelligence Engineering, modeling and application becoming rapidly advanced after each next day and in near future as Artificial Intelligence peak Bionic Brain and Humanoid Robotics which are at present also satisfactory but as will reach to Human-like qualities, features and traits in near future mankind will start to expect Humanoid should have to behave, act, response and feel like human beings. At this point Artificial Intelligence and DeepMind designers switching modeling and development to engineer "Feeling in Robots or most precise in Humanoid can be possible to engineer Neural Schemas as exact mimic of Human "Natural Emotion" in the form of "Virtual Emotions" in Robots/Humanoid. When technology hit to height saturation will occur of Artificial Intelligence and the term called "Singularity". When singularity occurred at this stage of A.I engineering Robots will become thousand times smart, accurate and power than human. In that era of Human verses Humanoid condition at present to predict is completely uncertain and toggle between whether Humanoid would be friend of Mankind OR treat Mankind as enemy though programming in our favor mankind code but deep learning and self-programming option can code oppose programs to our favor one. If future robots friends of mankind no issues but with reverse thinking if robots treat human as slaves or enemy than several major issues occur and also possibility of Human-Humanoid wars for their rights, laws, land, ethics, protocols and vice versa. The point in right words called "Robotics Violence". This happen with mankind only because we are giving artificial feelings like love, sorrow, happy, fear, joy, smile, cry etc. with programing neural schemas for 'Virtual Emotions" which tends to 'Artificial Feelings' in Humanoid or Robots. Hence we are responsible for next level of Artificial Intelligence with us how it will behave with us. This can be possible if we can able to program "Human Centric and Control Robotics Programing Against Violence (HCCRPAV)" [Term coined by Prof. (Dr.) Md. Sadique Shaikh]. The concept behind HCCRPAV is all A.I engineers, designers and researchers must engage themselves with keeping A.I Singularity and Robotics Violence in their minds and compile and develop such a single "Universal Program" which can destroy all kinds of Robots if seems to be with violence behavior, where to create such biggest program brainstorming and separate coding of each minor and major department of robotic violence possibilities need to code, compile, test and all the modules combine and compile as single human control anti-violence robotics program as single 'Universal Program' which can control or destroy any kind of harmful virtual emotions and artificial feelings of any kind of Robots/Humanoid using this single algorithm I coined and named the term as "Human Centric and Control Robotics Programing Against Violence (HCCRPAV)". It really time to glad world transforming digitally, virtually with full of 'Robotics Automations", but also equally point of fear and rethinking 'What if Robots control themselves automatically with self-programs'. The things is biggest question mark front of us and completely probable to solve. Hence as we are moving with advanced Artificial Intelligence tradeoff attention need to be pay on how to control if Robots or Humanoid become out of control. When think about Advanced Artificial Intelligence also think about Robotic Violence, Singularity and how to defense from Humanoid if it Violence or in mood of rule out to human civilization. Hence engineer and code Virtual Emotions and Artificial Feelings in Robots/Humanoid with precise human centric and instant control in human hand.

# Episode Twenty-Six: After Human: The World of Brain-Net on Earth

**Interaction:**

"The mind of man is capable of anything….because everything in in it, all the past as well as all the future [Joseph Conrad]".why I am using above quote and what is the relation to what point I am coining you will understand its relevant your own as you moving line by line of this write-up. This topic though complex to some people to get understand, but those has strong or at least average background of Space, Physics, Quantum Mechanics, Neuroscience and theory of evolution definitely acquire it. Near distance and physical face to face communication started with the evolution of humankind and changes in each evolution in DNA structure caused to changes in communication patterns from different phonetics to gestures, gestures to voice and voice to voice with different languages. But first remote distance communication we can only considered to Post office Communication with written language on papers and remain long time one of the biggest but very slow source of remote communication from one person to another person, than after telegram and radio communication came in existence but fairly good and very expensive with charges per words in line to send from one person to another person. Great phase shift occurred in the world when electronic communication system successes with telephones and walky talky, pagers and satellite phones which are several times instant as compared to all mentioned traditional communication systems, but mankind not settled with this and computer and mobiles communication begin to rule whole world as very instant sources of communication with World Wide Web (WWW) called "Internet" of Computers further due to smart phones tends to Internet of Mobiles/Smart Phones. Since 1999 to 2013 "Internet of Computer (IoC)" boomed and with rapid and abrupt advancement of mobile phones which are equal or more powerful, accurate, fast and instant as compare to computers with high connectivity to WWW world shifted to next level "Internet of Mobile (IoM)" and lot of physical aspects even can say 35% physical aspects of human routine transformed to virtually or electronically using it. Since 2015 one term rushes in world called "Internet of Things (IoT)" and the concept is here all living things like Human, Animals and all can communicate using Ubiquitous Communication Network (UCN) and Radio Frequency IDentification (RFID) modules which is unique for each one connected in IoT across the globe. This technology further researches, engineered, refined and polished as what available at present with us in 2020 called "Internet of Everything (IoE)" where not only living creatures like, Human, animals, mammoths etc. but also 'Non-living' things like all automobiles, transportations, buildings, furniture's, consumers and kitchen and home appliances, almost everything of entire world connected in UCN with their unique RFID. Now the next two levels with connections possibilities I am explaining here after World Wide Web (WWW) next two are Planets Wide Web (PWW) where all planets of our solar system or interstellar space can communicate with each other with human and other alien's civilizations. With further expansion Universe Wide Web (UWW) where all Universe planets, asteroids, moons, stars and their aliens civilization can communicate with each other also with mankind but when this happen human changed its present form due to the change in human DNA structure which vanishes all human body parts and organs which mankind not using since long time. Analogically you can take example of your computer or smart phones the software's or files those you are not using since long time operating system sac you to delete or remove all unused. Because of advanced Artificial Intelligence and automation human using machines for their minor to minor or major to major work instead of body parts like hands, legs, eyes, mouth etc. therefore DNA structure will start to remove all unused body parts of human and finally the main processor "Brains" left in entre world with brains civilization instead of human civilization. In USA, Japan and China already research success and reach to next level to connect one human brain with another human brain using sensors and actuators advanced electronic/optical A.I based communication network and data/information from one brain to another brain directly possible to send without typing and speaking a single word of language using modulation and demodulation of thoughts or fired neurons schemas as transmission and reception frequencies or thoughts frequency. After human or after human body is just a brain with vanished all body parts and connected across the world with each other with "Thoughts and Consciousness" of human brain. Now if such would be happen that what about human 'Sex and Population' how mankind reproduction to sustain its identity because if only brain left in world as after human form which are "Unisex" I.e. all males and females brain are same in nature and unisex hence how reproduction possible in that case every Brain create its Clones Brain as its family. All brain directly +transmit and receive data/information, copy data/information or uploads downloads data, information, files , delete or modify, update date/information from one brain to another brain with ultra high instant communication speed called this ultimate network "Internet of Mind " or "Brain-Net". Perhaps this Brain-Net also we can say "Net of Consciousness" where all past, present and future already in brain which reflect outside as illusion what we call our "Reality". Here analogically you can take example of Electronic projector or Holographic projector where everything is processed inside projector and what observe outside is just reflections of lights with different refractive and reflective index in the form of pictures or motion pictures but if you want to touch it physically you won't. Similarly everything processed inside Brain as consciousness and out as Reality front of our eyes for our eyes and through/by our eyes. In last I would like to remark that Everything the World, The Universe, The Multiverse, Human Relations, Love, Religions, Wealth, and all are just a "Consciousness" of Brain with different pattern of "Reality Illusions" projected out from our brains to see everything with different "Perceptions" likes and dislikes called "Mind" and to control and educate it called the "Wisdom" of Mind. Hence "Brain-Net" would be "Net of Consciousness (NoCon)" with WWW, than PWW and ultimately UWW communication network technologies in future up to the year 5020. But off course I admit The God exist, the power who created this consciousness with illusions ability in Human Brain. But Consciousness has no religions, no belief or ideology, no gender, no sexuality, no race, no age and no nationality. You ARE Consciousness…therefore pray to the power not picture and live in future with "Internet of Consciousness (IoCon)".

# Episode Twenty-Seven: Global Pandemic "COVID-19 (Corona-Outbreak)" as "Change Agent" for Digital Transformation of World

**Interaction:**

The world progress itself witness of after each Pandemic on mankind world changed or shifted to next level in life styles, technology, transaction, trading's and all walks of life to protect and progress with high defense to such a Pandemics occurred in history to paradigm shift and phase shift of Human Civilization with all Money, Materials, Cloths, Homes, Educations, Foods, Medicine, Bank, Hospital, Shopping and likewise all aspects of life for "World Transformation" with available best technology o in that present time in history after each pandemic on planet earth for humankind from stone age to mechanical, mechanical to steam, steam to electrical and electrical to electronic and optical right now. Hence can conclude each occurred pandemic behaves itself as "Change Agent" to transform world and human civilization to next improved and advanced level using present technology of time and COVID-19 is one the biggest pandemic occurred at the end of 2019 and covered complete 2020 and exactly as I stated became Change Agent to transform world activities and human civilization to next advanced level using presently available technology, and is "Digital Computing, Electronics, Advanced Artificial Intelligence and Internet of Everything (EoT)  and advanced optical communications system.  COVID-19 not only effect on human lives and mental condition or psychology but also affect all their routine lives, businesses, academics, banking, economics, jobs and bread and butter. Now a days we can also able to say that COVID-19 became "Theme of Fear" on planet earth , because virus not spread out in air but spread out with human-to-human transmission with touch and contacts. Therefore social distancing and lockdown only solutions with governments across the globe to get protect from Corona Virus. Hence this the point of turning to collapse all physical activities to avoid human contact and transform all activities "Virtually". Thus government has taking to discard all physical processes and activities in all aspects and routines and necessary to mankind Banking, Hospital, Shopping, Education, Transportations Bookings, Businesses, Transaction, Trades, and everything and transformation of them Electronically or Digitally in nice word "Virtually" with the help of advanced technologies like, Advanced Computers, Cloud Computing, Servers, Bigdata, Internet of Everything (EoT), Advanced Artificial Intelligence, Advanced Communication System, Smart Phones (Mobile) and their supporting user-friendly and interactive Web-process, Software's, Mobile Application etc. Before COVID-19 number of virtual users across the world around 37% which are after COVID-19 facts and figures to above 70%. Hence even if small to small transaction or activity or major to major people doing them digitally, therefore we are very near to transform all our routine physical activities with all walks 100% virtually up to 2030 and that would be also End Point of Physical Currency/money. The world even not only stay with adapting these technologies because already researcher succeeded their research on "Internet of Mind (Brain-Net)". Where human thoughts directly converted in frequency (Signals) and transmit from one to another remote brain using "Brain-Net". In last I would only like conclude this present pandemic changed several things and in process of changing several things and those would be very instant, secure, safe, accurate and with human comfort zone and will reduces buildings burdens for Shops, Business, hospitals, medicals, colleges, institutions, bank, schools, and all aspects, reduce Air pollution because of work or anything from home in near future due to low traffic on roads, reduce noise pollution, money or currency physical form vanish and only become figures and integers in bank accounts and many more things will get change only governments has to implement everything with strong brainstorming, forecasting and Vision.

## About Book:

This book not only a scholarly monograph but a quick journey to future with Artificial Intelligence with my modelling, vision, forecasting, perspectives and modern approaches. All the concepts, contents and models as book write-up I wrote in very easy language to understand by one and all levels of reader's which left you speechless after reading this book. I tried my best to create full-fledged Ethiopia of Artificial Intelligence with all its positive, negative and controllable impacts lucidly. Hence the book not only for AI engineers, practitioners, researchers and designers but also for all general readers who are interested in Present and Future of Artificial Intelligence.

## Author Brief:

Prof. (Dr.) Md. Sadique Shaikh is one of the outstanding contributor in the field of Advanced Artificial Intelligence and coined several new terms, concepts, theories and models in AI. He has qualified M.S(ES), M.Tech (IT), MBA (HRM), MBA(MM), PGDM, DBM, M.Phil., DMS(IBM) followed by Ph.D. he is at present Director AIMSR, he is international author/speaker and scientist. He has published 61 international books more than in 9 international languages, 123 research papers and 120 conference papers.

Publisher: Eliva Press SRL

Email: info@elivapress.com

**Eliva Press** is an independent publishing house established for the publication and dissemination of academic works all over the world. Company provides high quality and professional service for all of our authors.


Our Services:
Free of charge, open-minded, eco-friendly, innovational.

-Free standard publishing services (manuscript review, step-by-step book preparation, publication, distribution, and marketing).
-No financial risk. The author is not obliged to pay any hidden fees for publication.
-Editors. Dedicated editors will assist step by step through the projects.
-Money paid to the author for every book sold.  Up to 50% royalties guaranteed.
-ISBN (International Standard Book Number). We assign a unique ISBN to every Eliva Press book.
-Digital archive storage. Books will be available online for a long time. We don't need to have a stock of our titles. No unsold copies. Eliva Press uses environment friendly print on demand technology that limits the needs of publishing business. We care about environment and share these principles with our customers.
-Cover design. Cover art is designed by a professional designer.
-Worldwide distribution. We continue expanding our distribution channels to make sure that all readers have access to our books.

**www.elivapress.com**

www.ingramcontent.com/pod-product-compliance
Lightning Source LLC
Chambersburg PA
CBHW071549080326
40690CB00056B/1611